HISTORICAL GOLD COINS OF MUGHALS

HISTORICAL GOLD COINS OF MUGHALS

Satya Pratap Singh

ISBN: 978-93-5128-039-2

Third Edition, 2014

Published by

Kalpaz Publications
C-30, Satyawati Nagar,
Delhi – 110052
E-mail: kalpaz@hotmail.com
Ph.: 9212142040

Laser Typesetting: Gyan Print (AB-I)
Printed at: G. Print Process, Delhi

Cataloging in Publication Data--DK
Courtesy: D.K. Agencies (P) Ltd. <docinfo@dkagencies.com>

Singh, Satya Pratap.
Historical gold coins of Mughals / Satya Pratap Singh. -- 3rd ed.
p. cm.
ISBN 9789351280392

1. Gold coins--India--History. 2. Art, Mogul--India. I. Title.

DDC 737.4954025 23

Dedicated to

My Son

Dr. Sharad Satya Chauhan

My Daughter-in-law

Smt. Vishal Chauhan

and

My Daughter

Sapna Ajay Singh Pathania

Contents

Preface

Every civilisation leaves behind it a rich legacy of thought, art, culture and artefacts. Although many a civilisations are extinct now yet their impressions on the sand dunes of time is etched permanently which always act as a catalyst for inspiring strength of the posterity.

In Asia, India and China have a rich legacy of their ancient civilisation and no wonder these two Asian giants are re-emerging in global economic and political scenario.

Thoughts, Art, Culture and artefacts are manifestations of any civilisation. We have also seen that thoughts and culture travel across the world unhindered and geographical or political boundaries have no relevance to this phenomenon. To demonstrate the relevance of my opinion, let me quote the excitement of 'ROBERT OPPENHEKMER', the nuclear scientist Director of the atomic explosion in the USA during the second World War. On completion of the successful explosion of the atomic bomb at the test site at LOS ALAMOS, he recited verses from the Bhagvad Gita (the song divine) and compared the explosion with the *Virat Swaroop* (cosmos which Lord Krishna had revealed to Arjuna in the battlefield of *Kurukshetra*.

We have a rich past for which we are genuinely proud of. The chapter of Mughal history is equally fascinating. Although the Mughals came as invaders in search of greener pastures in India yet they made India their permanent home. Akbar the great Emperor of Mughal dynasty married an Indian Princess to integrate their alien, identity with the Indian social fabric. He did not stop at that and propagated *Dein-e-Elahi* a unique concept of synthesis of the religious diversities. Akbar was a genuine securlarist and even practiced *Surya Namaskar* (Salutation to Sun God). Dara Sikoh, yet another Crown Prince and son of Emperor Shahjahan even translated *Upnishad* in Persian Language.

I have no pretence of being a historian or an expert on art and culture and have recapitulated the few glimpses of history since it has the direct relevance on the core theme of my investigation as the title of the book would suggest. A valid question could be asked as to what is so special about the coins so as to warrant our attention. My answer is simple because these coins are an integral part of our historical and cultural heritage and we cannot be a mute spectator as these coins were stolen or embezzled and taken out of India with a view to auction them.

I would also like to ask a very valid question that as to who would believe us if we say that the Taj Mahal was built by the great Emperor Shahjahan, if the magnificent edifice which is one of the seven wonders of the world was not to be found on the ground. Seeing is believing and million have seen and continue to visit Agra. Many Western scholars think that great literary epics *Ramayana* and *Mahabharata* are the work of fiction and some of our own pseudo-intellectuals have joined the bandwagan and refuse to believe that a bridge between the southern tip of India and Ceylon was constructed which is popularly known as *Ramsetu* to facilitate the advance of army of the Lord Rama to Lanka:

> A few comments on investigative effort too are needed. No nation can survive without having a robust, healthy and well-oiled intelligence apparatus at its disposal. Intelligence craft has therefore been used since time immemorial to preserve, protect and promote the interests of a nation. But for his superior intelligence network, Rama could not have secured victory over Ravana since his army had much superior weapons in comparison to monkey army who had to fight with primitive weapons like stones and branches of the trees. This phenomenon is repeated in 'Mahabharat War' too where the victory of the Pandava's was possible because an elaborate network of intelligence machinery of Lord Krishna by which he successfully neutralised star-studded military commanders of the Kauravs. Coming closer to our history, we witness

Chanakya who in the 3rd Century BC, threw the corrupt and inefficient dictator from the throne of the Magadh and installed an unknown Chandra Gupta Maurya who ultimately became the Emperor of the unified India in due course.

The technology and methodology now available to our intelligence organisation is too advanced and sophisticated, notwithstanding these developments, the human mind shall always predominate and will be the crucial factor in any successful outcome of an investigation endeavour. But any investigative effort is like mounting an elephant where we have nothing in hand to control the elephant except for a small tool called *ankush*. But this elephant is a strange creation made of personal prejudices, unwarranted extraneous pressures and at times inducements which in its totality are more deadly than a berserk elephant. There are strong reasons to reduce the investigative journey in the book form for the following reasons:

(i) The two gold coins, the subject matter of the investigation is an invaluable wealth of our historical and cultural heritage. Although the auction of these gold coins was thwarted by the sincere and bold efforts of our Government in 1987, and yet these are likely to figure in an auction sometimes at a later period of the history.

(ii) We do not want our future investigators to enter the dark tunnel in case these coins appear for auction later. Sufficient ground has been covered, missing links have been joined and a very clear picture has now emerged which can be used as invaluable reference material in the future.

(iii) As the story unfolds in the succeeding chapters it brings out vividly as to how the greed and unbridled ambitions of a few individuals can tarnish the image of a well-respected ruling dynasty.

To sum my arguments, I am tempted to quote an incident from the great epic Ramayana. When the monkey-army of Lord Rama was constructing the *Ramsetu* (now called Adams bridge) a squirrel was noticed making an effort to help the task force of the engineers. On being questioned the squirrel replied that she too wanted to contribute in constructing the bridge. She was not only ridiculed but brought to Lord Rama for necessary admonishment since she had deeply injured the ego of the monkey-army by her humble utterances. Lord Rama was deeply touched by the gesture of the 'tiny creature' and blessed her by affectionately patting her back. The incident is still alive in our folklore and it is said that strips on the back of the squirrel are impressions of the Lord Rama's fingers. I think it would not be prudent to make more explicit confessions and expose my incompetence any further.

I am reminded of an essay on culture and anarchy on protocol and social criticism by Mathew Arnold the eminent English poet and thinker who defines the culture as "sweetness and light". Devoid of these virtues we shall only push ourselves towards the animal world. The shining example of imbibing cultural legacy in the nation's psyche is our neighbour Indonesia although predominantly a Muslim nation, they have named their national career 'GARUDA' the aerial vehicle of a Hindu Mythological God.

Satya Pratap Singh

Acknowledgements

With a Deep Sense of Gratitude

I Sincerely thank:

1. Mr. M.L. Wadhawan, Former Director General, Central Economic Intelligence Bureau, New Delhi.
2. Director General, National Museum, New Delhi.
3. Director General, Archeaological Survey of India, New Delhi.
4. Director General, Andhra Pradesh State Archives, Hyderabad.
5. Director General, Crime Authority of Australia.
6. Financial and Advisor to Late Nizam, Hyderabad and David Devdas and Amarnath K. Menon From India Today Bureau.
7. Mr. Shivendra Singh Rana, Former Commissioner of Customs Hyderabad and currently Director General Vigilance CBEC, Ministry of Finance, New Delhi.
8. Mr. P.K. Dash, Addl. Director General Revenue Intelligence, Mumbai Zone.

1

Mughal Era Rare Gold Coins

Listed for Auction

Auctions takes place all the times around the world but such activities hardly arouse an anxiety amongst us. When the artwork of any famous painter or the garments of a renowned actress fetch enormous prices, We do envy the riches it brings to the beneficiary because we do feel how useless creature we are. However, it is very seldom when an intended auction prick our consciousness and motivates us to do something positive to thwart such thing to happen because it amounts to molestation of our national heritage.

Two rare gold coins of Mughal era worth $ 14 million (Rs. 18 crore) were listed for auction in Switzerland on 9th November, 1987. The rare gold coins were offered for sale at a private auction at Hasburg Feldman in Geneva but the intervention by our Ambassador restrained the buyers to refrain from participating in the auction. To some extent the Global Stock crash at that material, time also created conducive conditions in our favour.

It may be surprising to many as to what was so special about these coins. In fact these were rare coins and an integral part of our history, culture and grandeur. One out of these two gold coins was at 11935.8 grams (approximately 12 kgs) in weight and of 20.3 centimeters in diameter. It was minted in Agra in the year 1613 AD by Mughal Emperor Jahangir.

The other coin of 9.7 centimeters in diameter weighing 1094.5 grams was minted in the year 1693 AD in Lahore by Emperor Shahjahan. These gold coins were made of pure gold with elaborate inscription in Persian and Arabic.

We have historical evidence in Tajuk-I-Jahangiri, Emperor Jahangiri's personal journal that he presented a coin (Mohar) of 1000 totals (roughly 12 kgs) to Persian Ambassador Zambi! Beg and yet another reference in lqbalnarna about such present to the Persian Ambassador. This fact is being brought to highlight the fact that the Mughal rulers had the tradition of minting such coins, but these historical facts had no relevance either to stop the auction or to bring back these coins to India unless we ourselves participated in the auction or purchased the coins directly from the auctioneer. Our Ambassador in Switzerland did make a very valiant effort to pre-empt the auction on the grounds that these were smuggled out of India. His request however, was turned down since it was not covered by the law of dual criminality. The reaction of the Swiss government was on the expected lines. I myself had bitter experience while investigating hawala transactions in Singapore and Hong Kong when our counterparts in these countries posed the counter question. So what "in response to our reasoning". In relation to these coins, matter was even more complicated since Switzerland is not a signatory to the International convention governing such claims by the signatory nations. Our luck was however, helping us as the bidders failed to respond to the reserve price fixed by the auctioneers. The auctioneers had no choice but to buy back the coins from the bidders at a much higher price from the bidders for the owners of these coins.

The Government of India was serious enough not to allow the opportunity slip away. Accordingly the Central Bureau of Investigation (CBI) lodged a complaint with the Interpol that these coins were stolen in India and sometimes after 1947 were smuggled out clandestinely. Since our complaints are duly covered the dual criminality clause. These coins were taken off the auction. The CBI plunged into action but there was yet another hurdle. The Andhra Government whose permission was mandatory to investigate the case in Hyderabad, for some un-understandable reasons refused the permission.

The solution to this unexpected roadblock was immediately found and the Government decided that the case be investigated by the Central Economic Intelligence Bureau (CEIB) an Intelligence Organisation in the Department of Revenue in the Ministry of Finance since no mandatory permission was needed from any State Government to investigate the case. I was lucky enough since the investigation was assigned to me. I was bit nervous since being a Revenue intelligence official, I had no formal training or experience to investigate a case of theft which was essentially a Police job. It however, dawned upon me that my first priority should be to establish the fact that Nizam was in possession of these coins and after having been stolen these coins were smuggled out of India sometimes after 1947, i.e., after India became an independent nation. A difficult task indeed owing to the historical gap of Mughal Era and emergence of Asifjahi dynasty popularly called Nizams of Hyderabad.

Although I was shaky to begin with but my army background comes to my rescue. We were taught on our very first day in the Indian Military Academy to be proud of our uniform and task assigned to us. Thus an uniform whether it is worn by a Military man or a police officer is not merely a designer's creation but it is a symbol of trust and faith which the nation reposes on the individual who wear the uniform. My initial intuition therefore quickly disappeared and I quickly got focussed and motivated to undertake my investigative journey.

2

The Philosophy of Minting the Special Gold Coins

Although we may never be able to decipher the philosophy of minting such gigantic cold coins by the Mughal rulers yet it is very interesting to make an effort in this regard. We must be very clear that these coins were not part of the usual currency used in day to day business transactions. As we know, Babur the Founder of the dynasty in India had made two unsuccessful attempts to capture Samarkand in Central Asia and therefore turned his attention to Afghanistan. Here too he could not make much headway since he had to face fierce and crafty tribal lords of the region. As a last resort he directed his military campaigns towards India. Such scheme of things was not in his agenda since he had fallen in love with beautiful hills and fruits of Afghanistan.

We may attribute the success of his military campaign in India because he took a wise decision to destroy all the wine caskets notwithstanding the fact that he was immensely fond of his drinks. His luck was however, shortlived and his pre-mature death brought Humayun to the throne. Misfortunes however overtook Humayun when Sher Shah Suri, an Afghan Chief who ruled some territory in Bengal dethroned him and he had to flee out of India. The luck however smiled again at him when Sher Shah was killed accidentally in an explosive blast at fort KALINJAR (Banda district in UP) when he was on a military campaign. Had it not happened the history of India may have been altogether different.

He retrieved his throne but his untimely death brought Akbar to the Mughal throne. Though Akbar was a minor and had no formal education owing to turbulent circumstances he was living in, yet he had extraordinary native intelligence and was assisted by the intelligent and trustworthy Ministers.

It was imperative to bring these facts on record so as to appreciate the philosophy of minting the special gold coins. As stated earlier it may not be fully possible to appreciate the practice of minting the special gold coins. To my mind, the primary reasons to initiate such practice had strategic, political and social considerations. The Mughal called these coins — Nazrana Coins (Souvenir coins) which were gifted to the visiting dignitaries to commemorate events like coronation or at any other special occasion. If we scrutinise the list of the recipients of these coins we find that the highest honour was always reserved for the visitors from the Persian countries. Apparently, they thought the biggest threat to their empire could originate from any of the ambitious Persian rulers and by gifting these coins to them, they achieved their strategic goal. These were also gifted to locals, as well as, to the visitors from neighbouring states to earn their goodwill so essential for the Mughal dynasty to take root in India and I shall demonstrate it further in the book.

The practice of minting special gold coins was thus started by Akbar but the, pieces minted during his reign did not exceed 102 tolas (one kg 183 gms). It may be owing to financial constraints as there were numerous military campaign which caused a severe burden on the exchequer. But Jahangir was more ambitious who struck gold coins weighing 500 tolas (five kg 800 gms) and 1000 tolas (11 kg 600 gms). Akbar was more keen to enhance the financial reserves so vital for the sustenance of the empire. The inventory of the treasurers taken after his death would bear testimony to this fact which are tabulated as under:

1. 272 mounds of uncoined gold (10850 kg).
2. 10 crore of rupees in the form of gold mohur coins of varying weight.
3. 370 maunds of silver (14800 kgs).
4. One maund of precious stones (40 kgs).

The practice of minting special gold coins continued till the reign of Shahjahan and it was Aurangzeb, who abruptly stopped the practice. It appears that the logistic lines of Aurangzeb owning to his campaigns in South India were too lengthy and to sustain his marching army he used to secretly bury the gold in advance of the marching route to avoid looting of the treasures by rising Maratha Power.

Contrary to popular belief the coins were minted, not only of gold but silver as well. It appears Emperor Jahangir had poetic bend of mind since he gave distinct names in each category of coins which are as under:

Gold Coins:

(i) coin of 100 tolas (equivalent to one kg 160 gms)–Nur Shahi

(ii) coin of 50 tolas (equivalent to 580 gms) – Nur Sultani

(iii) coin of 20 tolas (equivalent to 232 gms) – Nur Daulat

(iv) coin of 10 tolas (equivalent to 116 gm) – Nur Karam

(v) coin of five tolas (equivalent to 58 gms – Nur Mihir

(vi) coin of one tola (equivalent to 11.6 gm) – Nur Jehani

Silver Coins:

(i) 100 tolas (equivalent to one kg 160 gms) Kaukab-i-Tali (Star of Horoscope)

(ii) Coin of 50 tolas (equivalent to 580 gms)-Kaukab-I-Iqbal (Star of Fortune)

(iii) Coin of 20 tolas (equivalent to 232 gms) Kaukab-I-Murad (Star of Desire)

(iv) Coin of 10 tolas (equivalent to 116 gm)-Kaukab-I-Bakhi (Star of Good Luck)

(v) Coin of five tolas (equivalent to 58 gm) - Kaukab-I-Saad (Star of auspiciousness)

(vi) Coin of one tola (equivalent to 11.6 gm) - Jahangir 1 [(Fundamentals of Interrogation Techniques by Satya Pratap Singh, published by Gyan Publishing House, Delhi.)

The pertinent question before us how minting of these coins achieved the strategic political and social objectives of Mughal think-tank. As we know these coins were invariably minted at the time of coronation of the Mughal Kings and were gifted to visiting dignitaries from various Kingdoms. In doing so, the Mughal rulers were successful to ward off any external threat to their empire. Not surprising that there was never any invasion coming from outside India. The Gold coins of smaller denominations may have been given to various military commanders depending their rank, authority and influence on the masses. Similarly, silver coins which were cheap in value may have been given to people of lesser influence to win over their loyalty and allegiance to the Mughal throne.

There is however, no unanimity amongst the historians with regard to the real intentions of the Mughal rulers about the minting of these coins. Some English historians called them phenomenal coins and a few others as gigantic coins owing to their shape, size and weight. I have my own reasons to believe that these were *Nazrana* coins for two obvious reasons. Firstly, these were distinct from the ordinary coins used in routine commercial activities. Secondly, because these were always given as a gift to commemorate the special occasions to the visiting dignitaries and also at times gifted to person who exhibited extraordinary courage and loyalty to promote and cement the strength of the Mughal empire in India. (The Nizam-History and relations with the British Government, by Henry George Briggs published by Benard Qijartitch in 1861) however, do admit that the word *'Nazarana'* does defy translation and we get only a fractured connotation of the word.

Giving away gifts on special occasions or during the exceptional circumstances have been prevalent in human society since time immemorial and continues even today. In modern statecraft, gifts are given in numerous other forms as well like financial aids, treaties and memorandum of understanding etc. The Mughal rulers achieved to a large extent their strategic political and social objectives minting and gifting away with these coins and achieved the summit of their glory besides bringing peace and prosperity to their subject.

The myopic views of Aurangzeb however, did not fit into the philosophical framework of the earlier Emperors and results thereof are known to every student of history.

3

Investigative Journey Begins

I was once interrogating a notorious smuggler of Narcotics who persistently either evaded the questions or gave a false reply. I impressed upon him that I knew everything nevertheless wanted that the truth should come out from his mouth. His reply was very revealing. Pat came the answer that a person should never tell lies to his doctor and a criminal should never speak the truth to the investigator. When asked as to what made him think that way, with a grin on his face, he said that both would prove to be fatal.

Interrogation is the other side of the coin of intelligence gathering and both are inseparable. Unfortunately, we have a deep-rooted bias against an investigating officer. People refuse to talk even if they know the facts of the case. Such difference always results in delay in cracking a case and the public interest are severely undermined. To put it bluntly, we are becoming totally immune and refuse to interact with the authorities and fail in our bona fide social responsibilities.

With adequate briefing, I was dispatched to Hyderabad (Deccan), once the capital of the Nizam's seat of Government. With a view to achieve some anonymity to execute my mission, I was authorised to make hotel arrangements of my choice and was also directed not to take any visible logistic support from the local revenue formations.

Sometimes very strange thing occur in a bureaucrats carrier way back in 1964, I was deputed to attend a three months course on fire-fighting in National Fire College which in those days was located in Delhi Cantt.

It was surprising because these courses are invariably reserved for officers from the ordnance and Army Service Corps. My roommate was one Cat. Haq from Army Ordnance Corps. This gentleman officer was an MA in Urdu literature from Calcutta University and we used to have very lively evenings. He generated an immense interest in me for Urdu poetry by revisiting poems of Ghalib, Bahadur Shah Zafar and Faiz Ahmed Faiz and explaining the importance of these poems in English for my benefit.

The luck again smiled on me when I was posted as a brigade intelligence officer in an Infantry Brigade in Tithwal Valley opposite Muzaffarabad (POK). The area was inhabited by Gujars (Shepherds) whose Lingua-franca was not Kashmiri but Urdu. During the four years of tenure with the Brigade I, acquired some proficiency to communicate my views in Urdu Language. This background helped me greatly in my investigation in Hyderabad since by speaking in Urdu I could establish an easy rapport with whom I was interacting to elicit information. The financial advisor to the late Nizam was highly cultured and helpful without whose co-operation I could not have moved an inch. In spite of these conducive circumstances, the staff of Nizam was not only loyal to the memory of their past ruler but they were very reticent to speak on the subject. I had to invent my own methodology to break the ice and earn their co-operation. I started dressing like a common man in *Paijama Kurta* and avoided to speak in English. I shared benches occupied by peons and chatted with them for hours. I could convince them that my mission was only to restore the royal treasure of the Nizam and nothing beyond. The strategy worked and at least I was able to win their confidence.

To begin with the following line of action emerged as the most pragmatic approach:

(i) To ascertain whether gigantic gold coins figured in any of the trusts created by the Late Nizam.

(ii) Whether these coins were reflected in any of the statutory returns filed by the Nizam like information furnished to the British Government under the defence of India Rules during the second World War or under the Gold Control Act.

(iii) Whether these gold coins figures in the records of the Nizam's office after joining the Indian Republic in 1948.

(iv) And lastly gathers the evidence of historical value as to how these rare gold coins travelled from the royal treasury of Mughal to the founders/rulers of the Nizam dynasty in Hyderabad.

To examine various options objectively it would be expedient to have the last Nizams immediate family tree which may be relevant and useful in our investigations. The composition of the family tree which may be relevant and useful in our investigations. The composition of the family of the late Nizam at the time of his death was as under:

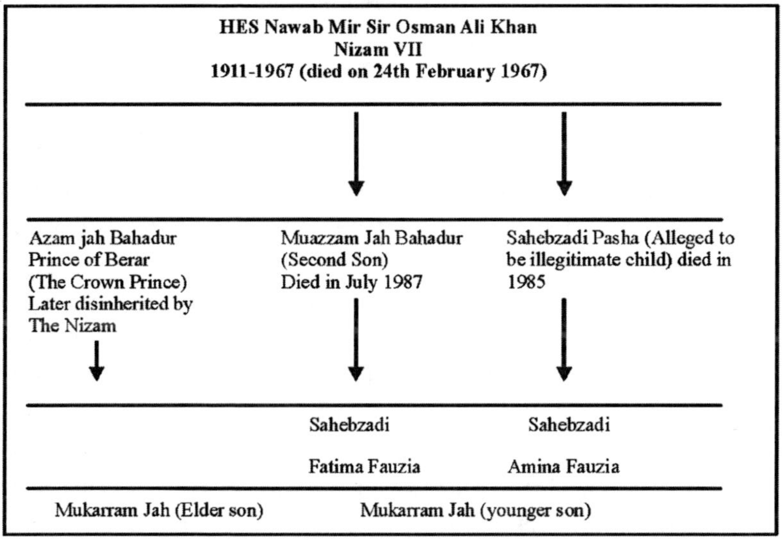

Mukarram Jah and Muffakam Jah were born to Prince of Berar from his Turkish wife. It is interesting to learn that the Nizam's, with few exceptions, invariably married their male heirs in Turkey unlike the Mughal rulers, who never looked back to Samarkand (Central Asia) for matrimonial alliances, Mukarram did his post-graduation from Cambridge University while Muffakam did his post-graduation from Oxford. As was the practice in Princely states in India Mukkaram also graduated from the Royal Military Academy at Sandhrust in England. It may be owing to this background he was crowned as Nizam VIII on 6th April, 1967 after the death of Nizam although by now the title was only a symbolic value than anything of substances.

Let us now examine which all trusts of precious treasures were created by Nizam.

1. *His Excellency Nizam's Jewellery Trust:* This was created in 1951 and contained 107 items including Jacob Diamond. The Government assessed the value of these trusts in March 1985 and 30 items were declared antiques by the archeological survey of India. Declaration were filed by the Trust in July 1971 with appropriate authority under the Gold Control Act 1967. Initially there were 45 beneficiaries out of which majority of them have died. Mukrram Jah however, continues to benefit maximum since he also inherits six per cent shares of the Late Nizam's younger brother who had no male issue and also that of Sahebzadi Pasha who died in 1985.
2. *His Excellency Supplementary Jewellery Trust:* This Trust was created in the year 1952 and 144 items were listed in it. This trust was created with a view to benefit the ladies of the family and also to members of the Nizam family in distress.
3. *His Excellency Jewellery for Family Trust:* The Trust was created in the year 1952 primarily with a view to assist members of the family in distress and contained 203 items. The entire assets however, were sold out in the year 1979.
4. *Sahebzadi Anwar Begam Trust:* This Trust was created in the year 1953 and contained 16 items. Part of it was given to her in marriage and the rest sold in 1979.
5. *Wedding Gift Trust of Nizam's Two Grand Daughters:* This Trust was created in 1951 for the benefit of two grand daughters viz., Fatima Fauzia and Amina Fauzia and contained 64 items.
6. *Sahebzadi Kulsum Trust (Grand-daughter):* The Trust contained 34 items and was created in 1953.
7. *Prince Muazzam Jah Trust:* The Trust was created in 1953, and only 12 items were listed in it. Jewellery of this Trust has already been sold out.
8. *Wedding Gift Trust of Nizam's Two Grandsons:* The Trust was created in 1951 however, the jewellery listed under it was sold out in the year 1972.

In addition to these Trusts Nizam wanted to create another Trust, viz., Muazzam Jah Trust for the benefit of the family. The Government of India insisted that Trust deposited roughly Rs. 21:12 crore.

In Government securities to create the trust. To fulfill this obligation the part of his gold *asharfie* (coins) boxes were counted sealed in boxes and deposited with the Reserve Bank of India who got these melted and converted these coins into 10 tolas, 100 tolas and 1000 tolas (each tola over-weighing 11.6 gms) and were transferred to Central Bank of India I, reputed brokers M/s Karmally and Sons Bombay. The total weight of this gold was over four lacs grams (roughly 400 kgs). The net outcome of the scrutiny of the documents pertaining to various trusts and the gold later sold by public auction clearly indicated that the rare gold coins we were in search of, never figured in any of the documents of trust or in the gold sold by public auction.

All the initial setbacks were not only disappointing but frustrating as well. When an idea struck me. We all know that since time immemorial, the mother earth has been doubling up as a safe deposit vault for the valuable treasures of the rich. In fact it was not only the rich class but even the gentry with meager savings indulged in such practice to safeguard their wealth from the theft and robbery. The practice is still in vogue in rural areas the banking system has yet not reached the remote and inaccessible areas.

When we talk about the ruling class of those days where wealth is strewn all around and accounting is a tedious job, the possibilities of theft and embezzlement increase many folds. After all greed is the major catalyst of all economic crimes and immediate family members and kins are the first to develop inclinations of such insatiable greed. No wonder the Kautilya the 3rd century genius of state-craft mandated payment of the monthly salary to various relatives of the King which included even the Queen whose monthly salary was equivalent to that of the Chief of the Army. It was the safest way to safeguard Kings wealth from misappropriation. It was quite possible that Nizam was aware of such human falling and may have constructed secret vault within the palace to store precious treasures secretly.

In the light of these facts it transpired that the architects of the palace could provide some leads in our efforts. It was interesting to learnt that in the Princely State of Hyderabad there were two kinds of architects. One category was employed in the State duties and the other category was exclusively assigned to the design and construction of any kind within the palace and they were designated as "In the personal service of the Nizam." We were successful in locating HARM OS CAWASJEE, aged about 85 years who lived in a parsee compound behind the Stanely Girl school, Gun Foundry Hyderabad. He was in very pathetic condition and his poverty was too evident to go unnoticed. It was quite ironical as well since the gentleman was an architect in the personal service of Nizam from 1926 till 1967. Another surprising fact was equally interesting as he was the life member of the Numismatic Society of India and had a few papers published to his credit on antique coins. I was unable to understand as to why his knowledge of Mughal Coins was sketchy and his answers were evasive. Apparently, it appeared to be deliberate. Since I was accompanied by Financial Advisor of the late Nizam. Considering his age, poor living conditions and threat to his personal safety in case he spilled the beans, his reluctance to co-operate was understandable. History always unfolds in very strange and unpredictable ways as I am tempted to share my experiences with readers which runs as under:

> I was investigating a case involving a violent encounter between the smugglers and Custom Officers in Jaipur Customs Collectorate. The clash had taken place near Jodhpur. When I arrived in Jodhpur in the night I requested the auto-rickshaw driver to take me to some decent hotel and he took me to the Ajit Cottages. A gentleman in short and tee shirt was at the reception desk and he allotted me a room baring No. 10. I refused to take this room and told the receptionist that No.10 denoted a criminal and he should allot me some other room. He was taken aback and asked me as to which clan of the Rajputs I belonged to. On being informed that I was a Khichi Chauhan he allotted me a self-contained cottage. I was deeply disturbed because my meager financial resources hardly allowed me to enjoy the luxury of a cottage. On the following morning, he introduced me to his lady wife whom he fondly called Chhoti

> Rani Sahiba (younger queen). I was surprised to learnt that he was none other than the younger brother of Maharaja Jodhpur who was acting as a receptionist just to pass his time.

I had learnt from my elder brother Dr. M.P. Singh an academician of repute in Delhi University that our ancestors had migrated from a village called Indroka in Jodhpur few centuries back to Uttar Pradesh in search of the better avenues in life. My visit to the village was arranged and it was the most emotional and the happiest occasion of my life.

While checking out from the hotel I was not presented the bill. I enquired from the younger brother of the Maharaja for this extraordinary generosity and he narrated to me the reasons in detail. I cannot vouch for the historicity of the facts but the story runs as under:

> During the Mughal period of history, the then Maharaja of Jodhpur was the contemporary of Emperor Aurangzeb. The Maharaja had two infant male children and Aurangzeb had an evil eye to annex the Jodhpur Kingdom in Mughal Empire by eliminating the Maharaja secretly. On a flimsy pretext, he requested the Maharaja to proceed to Afghanistan to suppress the revolt by certain tribal lords of the region with a view to get him assassinated. The maharaja proceeded to the battle zone with the entire paraphernalia along with the Queen and his two infants.

In those days the, Queens with a view to retain their youth and beauty never breast fed their children and the responsibility was given to the ladies of the other Rajput Clans. These ladies were called foster mother or *'Dhai Maa'* (Synonymous with Mother) in local language. The inner most security ring was also drawn from the husbands of these *'Dhai Maa'*.

While returning after the successful military campaign, the Maharaja of Jodhpur was killed by the trusted men of Aurangzeb but the inner security ring of the Maharaja succeeded in extricating the two infants and galloped towards Jodhpur. One infant died en route owing to strenuous journey but the other who survived was immediately crowned as the king of Jodhpur. Maharaja Ajit Singh further said the existence of Jodhpur State was primarily because of the courage, selfless service and devotion to duty of the Khichi Rajputs, who formed the inner security ring of the king and therefore there was no question of presenting a petty bill to a Khichi Chauhan.

I found a similarity in the fate of a CAWASJEE and residents of Indroka. They themselves could have installed their own leaders as the future king. History may not have been kind to the Khichis but their sacrifice will always remain etched with the glory in pages of the History of Jodhpur.

I had no heart to prove CAWASJEE any further on the subject and withdrew silently from the Pastawala compound.

4

From Deccan to Delhi

The Central Government was very serious to ensure that the gigantic coins listed for auction were repatriated to India. With that end in view of the high powered committee was constituted to monitor the progress of the investigation. Besides the Secretary Culture as Chairman of the Committee, Secretary to the Prime Minister, Director General of National Museum were their members. The Central Economic Intelligence Bureau and the Central Bureau of Investigation were also taken on board and both the investigating agencies were directed to work in close co-operation to ensure smooth progress in the case.

I had a very strong inclination that the Director General, National Museum could be of immense help to me, since before taking over the National Museum he was Director of the National Gallery of Modern Art. In fact, it was he who was solely responsible to ensure the treasures of the Nizam of antique value were retained by the Government when these were listed for auction in 1979. It may be recalled the treasures of the late Nizam were displayed by the national Museum for public viewing in October 2001 amid tight security. It contained 173 pieces out of the 325 articles which were acquired from the jewellery Trusts of Mis Osman Ali Khan, the last Asif Jahi Nizam of Hyderabad. The articles displayed also included Jacob diamond whose current value alone is roughly 400 crore. It may surprise many that this diamond was initially not treated as an antique but laborious research and painstaking efforts by Dr. L.P. Sihare ensured that we have the seventh largest diamond in the world.

Dr. L.P. Sihare besides being a scholar of repute was also a gem of a person and down to earth in his approach. He never exhibited his scholarly exploits and had a childlike innocent smile and curiosity to put others at ease.

He informed me that such special and rare Gold Coins of Mughal era were with London Museum and probably also with the Asiatic Society of India in Mumbai but these were of lesser dimensions and weight. He was fully aware of the Mughal tradition of minting the gigantic Gold Coins which they termed as *Nazrana* (Soveneur) Coins but was not aware whether Nizam was in possession of such coins because Nizams were very private persons and secretive to the outside world.

When the erstwhile Princely States acceded to the Indian Union after India became an independent nation all these states had to file a statement of their wealth which included jewellery, precious metals, precious stones and also heir looms, etc., in the Home Ministry in a section called Inter State Department. Although this section is virtually non-functional but the information furnished by the erstwhile princely State is carefully stored. The Hyderabad State did not make even an implicit reference that they were in possession of and special Gold Coins of Mughal Era. I am told that under the Defence of India rule during the Second World War, even the Princely States had to declare the wealth in their information but even at that time also no such coins were reflected in their information. The present Gold Control Act of 1968 derives its strength from this very Defence of India Rules.

It was realised that our line of investigation hitherto was very passive which was primarily based on the statutory information submitted by the Nizam to the Government. It was therefore felt that a more aggressive approach be formulated by resorting to creation of moles within the family since information obtained from the insiders is bound to be not only accurate but useful as well in our efforts. This could be done by purchasing the information but it has discarded keeping in view the rich status of the extended family of the Nizam's as the purchase price of such information was bound to be very high. As a matter of rule such hypothesis is apparently true but there are exceptions as well as my own past experience would reveal which I would like to share with enlightened readers. The incident happened when I was the Brigade Intelligence officer way back in the year 1968.

In pursuance of a strategic goal I was directed to create a mole in the camp of the army deployed against us. Informers in these hostile environments are usually double agents and thus one of my informers succeeded in creating a mole for an active interaction session with me. I do not know how he had succeeded but it appears he may have floated some convincing story to his superiors to meet me and may have had his own malafide designs. This was too obvious as we examined his pre-conditions of meeting me. He conveyed to me firstly that he will cross over to the Indian side by using the cane bridge on River Krishna Ganga (Pakistani call it Neelam River) which was in existence but was never used as such. Secondly, he would pretend that he was on a mission of hunting wild animals in the jungle. Thirdly, soldiers accompanying him will be fully armed and none of my soldiers will carry any arms. The last conditions was that the alcoholic drinks should be served during the meeting.

It was a very risky proposal for any practical consideration. My Brigadier however, was a man of extra-ordinary courage and foresight and already had one posting as Military Attachee in Islamabad and had very good understanding of the mind of a Pakistani soldier. He gave me the green signal but put the entire brigade on operational alert to meet any unforeseen contingency. I, on my part along with my team was armed to the teeth but the weapons were well-concealed beneath the American Coat Parka which was part of our uniform in those extremely cold conditions.

The Rum started flowing liberally in a hut on the bank of River Krishna Ganga. The meeting lasted from 10 PM till four AM in the morning. I do not know what trick was played by my Gurkha Regiment body guards but my friend from across was unable to hold his glass. He forgot all his evil designs and parted away with the most sensitive information about his deployment. As a parting gift, I gave him one bottle of Old Smuggler Scotch Whisky since that was the only brand available in the Officers Mess in those days and Rs. 500 of Pakistani currency to the soldiers accompanying him as *Bakshish* (gift). On cross verification, we found the information divulged by him highly accurate. My informer told me later that the Pakistani Officer had a weakness for liquor and enjoyed drinking which was just not possible in their army. Such incidents are however, exceptions and not a rule but moles can be created in the higher echelons of any establishment provided the psyche of the man who is likely to be raised as a source is well-understood. I have withheld the name and rank of this officer with sole intention of saving this great soul from the ignominy of treason and humiliation of facing a court martial should he be there still alive.

In the light of such experience it crystallised that a mole could be created in the extended family of Nizam to solicit the information but creation of the right mole is a very tedious process and requires patience. It therefore, transferred that we should identify some disgruntled individual in the family and coax him to come out with the information we needed. If we analyse the family tree of the Nizam we know that Azam Jah, the Prince of Berar was disinherited thus Muazzam Jah, the younger son of the last.

Nizam should have been crowned as the VIIIth Nizam of the State but he was never considered for the honour because princess DURRASHAWAR, the wife of the disinherited son through her intrigues got him marginalised and it was Prince Mukarram Jah who became Crown Prince and was coronated as VIIIth the Nizam after the death of Nizam. The last Nizam was so biased against his younger son that no trust was created in the name of Muazzam Jah. As an after thought a Trust in his name was created with just twelve items in it. Although, Muazzam had died in July 1987, i.e., before our investigation began, it gave us the rays of hope that someone down the line carrying the baggage of humiliation would certainly come out to co-operate with us.

5

Hyderabad Again

To raise a reliable source is a very careful and laborious process which requires a lot of patience and periodic cross verification to ascertain his reliability. To raise an insider disgruntled person as a source for information is still more difficult. It is very rare that a Vibhishan (younger brother of Ravana) walks into Lord Rama's camp to seek asylum and then gives intelligence inputs to Rama from time to time ensuring destruction of Ravana's forces. Notwithstanding the virtues of Vibhishan's personal qualities even to this day he remains a symbol of deceit and is being despised.

To overcome the odds it was decided to seek the assistance of the local elites to reach upto the insider. It occurred to me that it could be achieved by roping in the influential persons from the media fraternity because they are focussed, motivated and very articulate. They have a tremendous capacity to thrust their ideas and convince others to fall in line. They have also a perfect Albi and thus have unhindered access to various strata of the society. It dawned upon me that it was "India Today" a fortnightly magazine published from Delhi who made the loud noises to draw the attention of scholars of art-treasure on all over the world and also of the Government to ensure that the stated auction of the Mogul era gold coins did not take place and the treasure is repatriated to India. Their role merits special praise because it was their single-handed effort and they could be victimised by the real and powerful stakeholders for their crusade.

My assessment proved to be correct and I found that my Journalist friends proved to be equally earnest and enthusiastic that the truth ultimately comes out. A series of meetings was held secretly and the working strategy was crystal clear by now the outcome of it which the readers will witness in the succeeding chapters, they did succeed in convincing an insider to co-operate with me. There was a caveat however to this working arrangement, that the sources would not reveal his name or identity, shall never meet me in person and pass on the information through my journalist friend. It was understandable since the informant was mortally scared to the individuals who perpetrated the crime.

While my friends were on the job, I embarked on the mission to ascertain as to whether the returns filed by the erstwhile Nizam state to the appropriate authorities under the Gold Control Act 1968 were factually correct in their contents when various jewellery trusts were created by the Nizam. To my good luck the local custom and central excise commissioner was headed by an officer under whom I had the proud privilege to work within 1971. He was very kind and equally enthusiastic to ensure that I must succeed in my efforts.

The scrutiny of the documents with Central excise authorities in Hyderabad, *inter alia* revealed that the declarations were made by the Nizam in February 1963 about the holding of the jewellery in numerous trusts created by him. Since these reports were not filed on the prescribed proforma and therefore same was again done in between July 1971 and 1974 in the prescribed format. The list of the items declared were carefully scrutinised which tallied, as mentioned in the documents of the trusts. Nizam's personal jewellery consisting of 834 items was also declared in prescribed proforma in August, 1972. The entire personal jewellery of the Nizam however was sold out later for Rs. 49 lakh and proceeds thereof were credited towards payment of the wealth and income tax. None of the returns from Nizam mention that he was in possession of the gigantic gold coins of the Mogal era. Whether such intention was unintentional or deliberate is also subject matter of our investigation. A senior officer of the Central Excise Commissioner on condition of anonymity however conveyed to me that the Nizam was in possession of rare gold coins of varying dimensions and weight which pertained to a different era of Mughal Rule, some of these coins even 21 kgs a piece. It appeared to me to be a false information since there was no evidence available to suggest that gold coins of 2000 tolas (23 kg 200 gm) were ever minted by Mughal rulers. Sometimes, we tend to form our opinion on the basis of floating, rumours and such opinions have no evidential value to buttress our claim to seek repatriation of the coins back to India.

In continuation of our efforts to gather solid evidence to prove that the Nizam was in possession of the rare gold coins it was considered expedient to meet someone who was associated with the Trusts of Nizam. It was gathered that one M.A. Ashraf was Secretary to Nizam's Trusts for a number of years. This person was found to be residing in Aziz Manzil opposite Kanchenjunga Building on King's Kothi Road. I was no match to the ingenuity of this 67-year-old man as he employed the ploy of hard of hearing and used a non-functional hearing aid to evade answers to my questions. Our interaction ended on a funny note, but his loyalty to late Nizam was really praiseworthy.

In the hours of my disappoint, a knowledgeable person suggested that I should visit the Andhra Pradesh archives. Frankly, I had no idea that such department could be of some help to me to that extent it was very useful information to me.

Andhra Pradesh archives are located at the outskirts of the city with idyllic surroundings. An ideal place for scholars to engage in quest of knowledge. The Director General of the Archives personally supervised the operation to dig out the information. It was a massive exercise since voluminous documents of the Nizam state had to be scrutinised. There was no reference in these documents with regard to gigantic gold coins of Mughal era. A well-informed officer in the archives however told me that, if at all, this information may have been shown in the 'SARFE KHAS STATE' (Nizam's personal estate) documents which in all likelihood may have not been handed over to the state archives by the Nizam. The officials, however, hinted that such references could possibly be found in the national archives since Nizam a: had acceded to the Indian Union after the independence. With a faint hope, I had to return reluctantly to Delhi to pursue my mission further.

6

From State to National Archive

I am really grateful to the sound advice of the Director General of State archives who convinced me to concentrate my efforts in the National archives, New Delhi. The Director General of Archeological survey of India and his dedicated staff went out of the way to ensure a happy end to frustrating journey. Visit to the National Archive gave me a soul-searching feeling after having experienced my ignorance of our vast and rich legacy of the past. After laborious efforts, we succeeded in locating a published work on Nizam titled "The Nizam His History and Relations with the British Government" authored by Henry George Briggs, who was an Indian Civil Service officer posted as the Secretary in Bombay Municipality. The book was published in the year 1861, but unfortunately the only first volume was available in the library. There was yet another hurdle to negotiate since the book was in the category of rare books and could not be issued to any individual. I had no option but to read the book in the premises of the archive. I was amazed to learn that such outstanding and carefully marshaled historical facts could come out of the pen of a bureaucrat and that who was an outsider with roots, thousands of miles away from India.

The effort really opened a Jackpot for me and missing historical links of a few hundred years between Mughal Era till the emergence of Asifjahi (Nizam dynasty) in India were easily restored. There is irrevocable evidence to the effect that gigantic gold coin of 1000 tolas 911 kg 600 gm) was indeed presented by Emperor Aurangzeb to the Father of the founder of the Nizam dynasty in return for the military services rendered by him to the Mughal Emperor. Aurganzeb was a very complex personality and that has no relevance to me except to the extent it has crucial bearing in our investigation. We knew that it was Aurangzeb who put a break on minting the special gold coins because he considered it a waste of the valuable resources which could be utilised in fulfillment of military campaigns for expansion of the Mughal empire. Gifting away the gigantic gold coins minted by his illustrious ancestors appears to be diametrically opposite to Aurangzeb's personality traits. He was a man of frugal habits and for his personal expenses instead of using the state wealth made copies of Koran Sharif for sale. But certain events of the history can compel any individual to discard such convictions and an Emperor could be no exception to such phenomenon. So to comprehend his such strange behaviour in its totality we have to peep into the pages of history during that period.

During the reign of the Emperor Shahjahan one person's name KHAJEH ABEED from Samarkand (Central Asia) visited the Mughal Court. He was a man of letters and a great poet. He was received by the Emperor favourably and was presented a dress of honour as well as Rs. 5000/- and was attached to the personal staff of the emperor. The poets, in these days, invariably accompanied military campaigns and using their poetic imaginations to the fullest extent highlighted the exploits of their kings. But unlike the poets of modern era poets of those days were great warrior as well. I, however, do find an exception in poet Nagarjun who was always slovenly dressed and projected dilapidated look. He was affectionately called Baba (a term of reverence) in the literary fraternity. To me, although he was a poet but seemed to be more of a warrior because he had conquered the materialistic desires of the word all by himself.

During the intervening period SHAHABUDDIN, son of Khajeh Abeed also joined the Mughal court and entered into the military services of the Aurangzeb. He acquitted himself admirably well in numerous military campaigns and Aurangzeb conferred on him the title of Ghazee-ood-Deen and later Firoz Jung. Thus, we see that the seeds of the Nizam dynasty in India were indeed sown by Emperor Aurangzeb which will be very evident from the succeeding paragraphs. During his military campaigns in South India— Azeem Shah, son of Emperor Aurangzeb was dispatched to Bijapur to annex it to the Mughal empire. Bijapur then was under the rule of Marathas. The Emperor himself camped at Sholapur to oversee the operations. Unfortunately, for him Maratha warriors succeeded in encircling Azeem Shah and all his communication and logistic lines were totally cut off. Leave alone the fodder for the horses of the army there was even acute shortage of food for the troops of the prince. He was constantly harassed by unexpected attacks from the Marathas and was facing total destruction. Even Emperor Aurangzeb was of little help to his son as there was an acute scarcity of food in his own camp at Sholapur.

Shahabuddin was a great tactician and he succeeded in breaking the cordon of the Marathas and restored supplies to the prince by carrying fodder and foodgrains in 20,000 bullock carts procured from Ahmednagar. Dulput Rao, a military commander of the Mughal army with his strong detachment secured the other flank. The Maratha warrior made a valiant effort to cut off the convoy of Shahbuddin and a well-contested battle was fought but the Marathas were defeated and the prince was rescued from utter destruction, defeat and humiliation. To express his gratitude one gold coin of the weight of 1000 mohurs (each mohur weighing roughly one Tola totally equivalent to 11 kg 600 gm) was sent as a present to Shahbuddin who was by now conferred the title of Khan Bahadur Firoze Jung.

This Shahbuddin was father of great Asif Jah who later founded the ruling house of Hyderabad. This is one of the gold coins listed for auction in Geneva in November, 1987 which is the subject matter of our enquiry. We find yet another corroborative evidence of the same in a book titled "Historical Studies in Mughal Numismates". By Hodivala which was published by the Numismatic Society of India in the year 1923. It clearly states at page 74 of the book that after the fall of Bijapur by the military action of Mughal army, Aurangzeb presented a mohur of 1000 tolas (11 kg 600 gm) to Firoz Jung. This gentleman is no other person but Shahbuddin, the father of the Nizam-I-Mulk Asif Jah, the founder of Nizam dynasty in Hyderabd.

We do not find any reference to the other gold coins of 100 tolas (one kg 160 gms) also in possession of Nizam rulers, the other coin which is also listed for auction. In no way, it weakens our case since in all likelyhood, it may have been presented to the ancestors of Nizam rulers as we do find evidence of gifting such coins to the visiting dignataries in events of even minor significance. There could be many reasons of such omissions. It could be bona fide human failing of the individual recording the evidence of such gift ceremonies. It could have been the deliberate direction of the Emperor Aurganzeb of the official recorded of the gifts as succeeding Para would suggest.

Khajeh Abeed was later killed in the seize of Golkunda (outer periphery of Hyderabad). In our opinion Khajeh Abeed in his life-time during his service of the Mughal must have been a victim of undue envy and jealousy of the other courtiers of the court because of his alien background and meteoric rise and influence in the Mughal Court and the Emperor simply wanted to shield him. Anyway, subsequent investigations do prove beyond doubt about the possession of this coin as well with the Nizam rulers.

7

The Last Nizam—The Melancholy Pesonified

Wealth alone cannot brings happiness. More often than that it can only invite misery. On the face of it, it may appear to be incongruent to my investigative efforts but surprisinng answers to my most complex questions came from the deep depression which the Nizam passed through during the last phases of his life.

While I was in Hyderabad, I decided that I should visit the palace of Nizam which is popularly known as King's *Kothi*. I, therefore, requested the Financial Advisor orally but he straightway rejected my request on the grounds that the *Kothi* was virtually locked and the caretakers and their families were the only habitants in the premises. Since the ladies were *'pardanasheen* (who despite being seen by outsiders) I could not be allowed to visit the *Kothi*. After sustained persuasion and on being convinced that the visit was only personal with a view to satisfy my curiosity about the life style of the erstwhile rules he yielded and agreed to escort me to King's *Kothi*.

In those days, there was hardly any literature on the Nizam unlike today. The latest book by JOHN ZUBRZYCKI titled the last Nizam. In fact the subject of the rise and fall of greatest princely state has drawn attention of Modern writers very recently. These writers have been basically travellers or administrators. It appears that most of the rulers of our princely states of the past had an impregnable cover of privacy around them which must have discouraged many authors not to approach them to pen their biography or life-style.

As we all know the last Nizam was a much maligned man and loads of anecdotes ridiculing him always floated in a gossip gatherings. Unfortunately, he has been victim of undue prejudice and bias. We should try to understand that personal inclination and idiosyncrasies do not sprout from a vaccum and there is a valid psychological background and also bona fide compulsions for such tendencies to develop in an individual over a period of time. It is unfortunate truth that he was perpetually unhappy with himself and with the persons of the family by whom he was surrounded all the time.

After the customary precautions that the privacy of the inmates was not infringed upon, I was taken to the King's *Kothi.* It was not a superimposing building as I had visualised about a Kings palace but a modest structure without any embellishments whatsoever. The palace looked deserted, 'unkept and gave me a feeling as if I was visiting 'a morgue'. The doors of the rooms were locked but since there were no curtains drawn. One could always peep into. I was thus able to walk in the corridors. There were lots of wooden almirah with countless files, wrapped in cloth and stacked upon them. Accidently, I spotted a book said to be authored by the Nizam, noticing my inclinations to possess the book, the financial advisor gifted it to me. As I could not read the Urdu script he read out certain portions of it and explained their contents. It was a book of poems really rich in contents and emotional intensity suffices to say that Nizam appeared to me as a highly gifted poet and therefore something about it later.

While walking in the *verandah* just outside the personal bedroom of the Nizam, I noticed a very strange thing. There were two footprints in the corner of the *verandah* which had deeply cut into the solid stone surface and were visible to the naked eyes even from a distance. On being asked as to what these two footprints were all about, the financial advisor informed me that the last Nizam used to stand at this very spot daily for hours and gaze into the sky as if he was searching answers to certain difficult questions. For over a period of two decades, he always stood at the same spot. I was also taken to various rooms of his *harem* (residential premises of concubines). Each room was open and one could easily visit the past, the Nizam lived in. Each room was in damaged condition. The sole occupant of the each room was now a broken piano, which was trying to convey the untold story. It left no doubt in my mind that the occupants of these rooms were not only beautiful but accomplished too.

I noticed yet another strange thing. In continuation of the *harem* quarters there were few self-contained cottages to ensure/comfortable living. To my query, the financial advisor informed me that whenever a child was born in the family, the mother was shifted to these cottages since Nizam hated the cry of a child as it disturbed him a great deal in his thought process. A very strange attitude but not surprising, since Nizam was a creature of unexplainable and strange proclivities.

I am inclined to recall an interesting anecdote which aptly fits into the state of mind of the Nizam. Once the great Mughal Emperor Akbar was on a routine round of the city to verify the welfare of his subjects, he spotted a beggar in the crowd. He was deeply moved and removed his costly necklace and gifted it to the beggar. After a week he was again on the same route and spotted the same beggar in the crowd. He got deeply annoyed and rebuked the beggar as to why again he had come for begging when during his last visit he had given him such a costly necklace that could ensure a comfortable living to many of his coming generations. The beggar politely informed the Emperor that he had not come for begging but to return the necklace and sarcastically told "*Jahapanah* (my lord how can you sleep with so much wealth around you." This incident may be true or otherwise but reveals the fact that the poverty always unites the people and it is the riches which splits even the most cohesive families. We all know why and how the epic war *Mahabharta* was fought. It was a question of only five villages although the Pandavas were the rightful owners of Hastinapur. It is therefore, not at all difficult to fathom the reasons for the loneliness and inner-turmoil of the Nizam. The abundance of wealth around and the greedy eyes of persons around him really tore him asunder.

It is established practice all over the world wherever the monarchy system of government was in existence that the second senior most person in the hierarchy succeeds whenever the king dies or abdicates the throne. It was therefore, natural that Muazzam Jah younger son of Osman

Ali Khan (the last Nizam) should have been declared heir apparent by Nizam instead Mukarram Jah, the grandson who was crowned after the Nizam's death. Although it was symbolic but the title 'entitled' such person for the entire immoveable and moveable wealth including heirlooms. The ongoing legal battles of ownership disputes of property in various erstwhile states are the results of undefined law but Nizam's family was in the battlefield even before the Nizam was gone.

We have no proof whatsoever as to how it happened but have reasons to believe that princess DURRASHWAR, daughter-in-law of Nizam and Esra, the wife of Mukarram Jah, both of Turkish origin must have coerced the Nizam to declare Mukarram Jah, the heir apparent who could succeed the Nizam after his death. The acrimonies bickering and malafide intrigues in the family must have saddened the Nizam deeply as he was still in the process of reconciling to the dramatic fall from grace owing to the historical events. No wonder, Nizam became an epitome of melancholy visualising the shadow of sad events approaching the family. It appears that Nizam was conscious of the manipulations and said consequences thereof. It is therefore, not surprising that he had appointed his financial advisor, who was not only a Parsee but a person from outside the state. The Chief architect who looked after the architectural requirements of the King's *kothi* was also a Parsee gentleman. His personal security consisted of Ansari's who were immigrants to the state. He was a paranoid man and constantly felt threatened). (It appears even the cry of an innocent new-born child was threatening him). Not surprising that he will stand on his two legs, motionless for hours and gaze at the horizon in pin drop silence.

The transformation in the personality of Nizam was on expected lines. From the truckload of titles which the British had conferred on him, he became an ordinary citizen of the Indian Republic which must have been very difficult to reconcile. To add salt to his injured ego, there was a coterie of close relatives who were all poised to betray him. It was his own family for his miserable isolation. The race to grab the wealth of the state had intensified and fall in the normal values of the siblings deeply pained him.

The visit to Kings *Kothi* had a very positive bearing on our efforts to ascertain the ownership of the rare gold coins by Nizam. It cemented by' conviction of cultivating an outsider with the help of my journalist friends. Howsoever, generous and accommodating one may be to the injustice and deprivations, he is bound to shake off the humiliation by exposing those who were responsible for his state of affairs. I got fully convinced that the insider will definitely reveal the details to me as to how the gigantic gold coins found their way to the auction table.

8

Nizam—The Generous Donor

Many may get surprised when I club the late Nizam in the league of the generous donors but it is not without reasons. I am aware of the facts that the Nizam was a much maligned man, and victim of countless prejudicial anecdotes portraying him the most miser man on the earth. Some gossip mongers even circulated the derogatory remarks that he used to smoke even the butts of the cigarettes left in the *ashtray* by the visitors. His humorous spat with Pt. Madan Mohan Malviya when he visited him for donations to raise the Benaras Hindu University is also well-known (B.H.U.) true or otherwise it can never be stated but he did donate a substantial amount for raising a university in Varanasi.

He understood and appreciated the value of the money. It may be true that he carried his convictions to illogical and ridiculous proportions but to condemn him on this count is equally blasphemous. No one can blame him although he had a dual face. He did not believe in squandering the public money on frivolous things and always applied stringent fiscal discipline on himself first. He was aware of the fact that the privy purse of Rs. 50 lakh (five million) by the Government of India to him was a public money because it was paid to him by the taxpayers. He smoked the Charminar the cheapest brand of the cigarettes in those days, never discarded his torn clothes but got them mended and discarded only those clothes which were totally irrepairable. No wonder during the state re-organisation in 1955, Telangana (erstwhile Nizam state) was the only self sufficient in comparison to other parts of the Andhra State.

The financial advisor with whom I was always accompanied narrated me the story that on completion of the police action in Hyderabad state when the Army General asked a person, who was loitering in the *verandah* of the King's *Kothi* as to where was the Nizam, the gentleman replied that he himself was the Nizam. He was so simple in his dress and at that material time was bearing only a Lungi (loin cloth) and *Kurta* (a stitched shirt used for covering the upper torso).

We are aware of the historical fact that Mehboob Ali Pasha, (VIth Nizam) the father of the Nizam because of his spendthrift habits had brought the state very close to bankruptcy and it was Mir Osman Ali, who not only brought the state finances on an even keel but also acquired wealth to become one of the few richest men, of the planet with a net worth of over 200 billion. We must therefore understand his time and circumstances and appreciate him than to ridicule for unilateral self-imposed poverty. If he was so miser how could he give so much to the state by way of infrastructure in the field of education, health and urban planning. It goes to the Nizam's credit that he neither made a Taj Mahal or a tomb to glorify himself but served the interests of the common man.

Hyderabad is one of the rare cities of India which boasts three universities besides other educational institutions. It was one of the most secular states where people of all religions, cast and creed could live in harmony and pursue trade, commerce and other activities. To say the least, it was one of the best administered princely state, the efficient governance requires money and for implementation of the developmental projects he led from the front by imposing financial discipline on himself and ironically we call such a man a miser.

In the wake of forced Indo-Pak war on us in the year 1965, the honourable Prime Minister Lal Bahadur Shastri not only gave the slogan of *Jai Jawan Jai Kisan* (glory to soldier and farmer) but also made an earnest appeal to all including Nizam to donate generously to augment the war efforts. The Nizam responded with grace and dignity and pledged a huge quantity of gold held in his possession. But for his generous donation, our investigation to prove embezzlement and theft would have a remained mystery forever and we could have never succeeded in preempting the auction of rare gold coins and their subsequent repatriation would have remained a dream.

Currently, there seems to be a positive debate by certain individual and groups regarding 'black money' concealed in the banks of tax haven countries. The perception and quantification of such wealth is however, in variance amongst individuals and groups. We all know that 'black money' in our country starts generating from the neighbourhood grocer's shop and is prevalent in any sale, purchase and any other business transaction. Thus, the concealed wealth contrary to the laws of the land is a 'black money'. Even if we succeed in bringing back the 'black money' from abroad, which is a Herculean task, no thought is being given to curb the generation of the 'black money'. It is deeply-rooted in our psyche and kings were no exception to such inclinations. These passing remarks have been made only to highlight the fact that the donation which was given in the shape of gold coins, etc., was indeed an undeclared wealth or black money with whatever name one may call it. The only difference being that instead of being deposited in foreign banks, the Nizarn's wealth was secreted in the secret vaults of the King's *Kothi*. This wealth was never declared by the Nizam in any of the statutory obligations incumbent upon him. In fact one of the pre-conditions of giving such a huge donation was that no legal action would be taken against them for concealment of the wealth and non-compliance of the mandatory laws.

In addition to the facts enumerated above there seem to be other compulsions rather more compelling. As the time was fleeting away the greed for misappropriating the vast riches of the Nizam was also intensifying amongst the members of the Nizam's family. Internal bickering, the trust deficit in each stakeholder of the family added to the frustration and mental agony of the late Nizam. As it is, he was already suffering from the acute guilt complex for cheating the government by concealing the wealth which at some point of time could result into a humiliating experience of fine, penalty and arrest if detected by the government.

He could not carry on with it any further, He rightly thought that the request by the Prime Minister was God sent as he could wash of his guilt and simultaneously secure a more honourable future of his family. He also thought that with no wealth around, the manipulations of the palace would also result in happy ending usherinq the family into cordial mutual relationship.

To achieve his goal, the Nizam informed the Central Government in December, 1965 about his decision to hand over his entire holding of gold coins weighing 425 kgs totally. This consisted of 15782 (to me it appears to be a deliberate misdeclaration to conceal the identity of two gigantic coins) and rare coins of numismatic value of *Asharphis* (resembling coins) and sovereigns. Nizam himself signed the letter addressed to the government. It will be interesting to note that the Nizam never signed any routine letters and job was left to the staff. In such drafts which were brought to his notice he did record his observation on the margins of the letter using the pencil. I was not inclined to believe this strange practice but this strange trait of Nizam's brought to my notice by a person who was a close confidant of the late Nizam.

Since Mr. Lal Bahadur Shastri, the Prime Minister unfortunately died in Tashkent, while he was in USSR to negotiate the peace deal with the President of Pakistan, the handling over the gold was unduly delayed. The gold was transported from the King's *Kothi* in October, 1966 at the residence of the Chief Minister of the Andhra Pradesh where the State Bank of India took over the gold on behalf of the government for safe custody and gave a receipt to that effect.

Now, let us see what was handed over to the State Bank of India contrary to the Nizam's commitment. Let us categorise what was pledged by the Nizam as a donation and what was indeed handed on the ground.

(A) Pledged	(i) 411 kg of solid gold (ii) 15728 in the form of rare gold coins some of them being of Numismatic value (iii) Total weight over 425 kgs.
(B) Handed over to State of Bank of India	411.6 kg solid gold.
(C) Difference between pledged gold and actually handed over	(i) 425 kg i.e., 425000 gms pledged (ii) 411.6 kg i.e., 411638 gms
(D) Viz. not donated but misappropriated during transit from King's Kothi to C.M's residence.	Minus 425000 411638 13.362 kgs

From the above table it is clear that the rare gold coins amounting to 15728 coins were embezzled and not handed over to the Govrnment. The weight of these coins comes approximately 13.3 kgs, i.e., approx 13362 gms.

Now, let us see what is the weight of the two gold gigantic gold coins listed for auction in Geneva.

(i)	Gold Coin minted in Agra by Emperor Jahangir in the year 1613 AD	11935.8 gms
(ii)	Gold coin minted in Lahore by Emperor Shahjahan in the year 1639 AD	1904.5
(iii)	Total weight	13.840 gms

It is surprising that the donors of the gold talk about the weight of the solid gold but are totally silent about the weight of the 15728 coins. Mystery of such silence is understandable. Actually, the minting of *Mohur* (coins) was started by the Mogul Emperors around 16th century and later British Rulers also used them as standard coins. The weight of these *Mohurs* (coins) used to be ten grams, five gram and one gram and weight of the coins was the intrinsic value of the coin. Now, it will be folly to assume that all the 15728 coins were of one gram each. Even if it were so, the minimum weight of 15728 coins should be around 16 kgs and not 13.362 kgs as the table suggests. Further, if the sole intention was to misappropriate the gold, it could have been from the lot of 411 kg of solid gold. Instead the entire lot of 15,728, gold was withheld.

It is therefore, clearly established that the two gigantic gold coins listed for auction in Geneva were part of the gold. Nizam had promised to handover to the Government someone embezzled it between the distance of Kings *Kothi* and the residence of the Chief Minister.

It may be ironical to club the Nizam in the category of generous donors but it certainly requires a big heart to part with a huge wealth of astronomical value which was part of precious treasures of the Asif Jah dynasty for a number of centuries.

9

And the Nizam Departs for His Final Journey

"When Beggars die;

No comets are seen;

Heaven themselves blazeforth,

The death of Princes"

So, said the great English dramatist Shakespeare. But unfortunately the VIIth Nizam died in very tragic circumstances betraying the prophecy of the great poet.

The behaviour of certain members of the Nizam family did hurt the Nizam very deeply that he could never recover from it. Lord Krishna in his song divine as revealed to Arjuna in the battle fields of Kurukshetra also forewarns us that the "aspirations generate greed which ultimately takes the shape of anger and this is the biggest enemy of mankind on this earth" (GITA- *Karma Yoga Shlok* 37). Nizam was a shattered man by October 1966, which rightly attributable to greed and evil aspirations of certain members of the family as the events unfolding within the four walls of Kings *Kothi* between December, 1965 and February 1967.

As we have already learnt that the Nizam had conveyed to the Government to donate little over 425 kgs. of undeclared gold to augment the war effort as early as December, 1965. This was however, not appreciated by certain key members not withstanding his best intentions to save the family from any future criminal liability. No wonder, the actual transfer of gold took place exactly after ten months in October, 1966. During the intervening period of ten months, there must have been acrimonies discussions and debates in the family against Nizam's decisions resulting in an inordinate delay in handling over the gold to the Government. I can visualise that the Nizam would have prevailed upon the delinquent successors of the family to honour pledge since the letter of the Nizam in December, 1965 clearly stated that it was unaccounted gold and never declared to any Governmental agency and same was being donated on the pre-condition that no legal action would be taken against the Nizam for their lapses willful or otherwise.

The bickering, deceit and betrayal by few individuals came out on the streets sooner than expected. The first question arises as to why the residence of the Chief Minister was chosen as a venue for transfer of the gold, when it could easily be done in the King's *Kothi* itself. Further, the Chief Minister really had no role to play in the event except that he was only a witness on this solemn occasion which he could have done even in the Nizam's palace. The answer to this question is too obvious. In case the gold had been handed over to the State Bank of India officials in the King's *Kothi*, the perpetrators of their evil designs could have never succeeded in the misappropriation of the historical gigantic gold coins in the presence of Nizam since he would have definitely witnessed the transaction.

To pre-empt such eventuality Nizam would have been coerced into accepting their suggestion of handing over the gold in the CM's residence. The transit time from King's *Kothi* to CM's residence was just sufficient to implement their plan and they did succeed since only solid gold of 411 kgs (411638 gms) was handed over and none from the lot of gold coins of numismatic value and *Asharfis* (coins). So far as the State Bank of India officials are concerned with only to accept the gold and give a proper receipt against the same to the donor which they did. It is only after the persons transporting the valuable treasures handed over the receipt ot the Nizam, the lightening of high-voltage betrayal struck him. He never expected that the persons whom he loved would be so cruel to him. It was a great blow to the person who ruled the kingdom with dedication and dignity to make, envy of other ruling houses. The tragedy had struck him so hard that he could never recover and started slipping into 'comma' gradually. It is further surprising that he was not admitted in any hospital either at Hyderabad or elsewhere although he could afford the costliest treatment anywhere in the world. It is also not known as to who was treating him in King's *Kothi* but we are certain that he was discreetly guarded by the personal security of Mukarram Jah. Ironically, Nizam could never realise in 'comma' that to those whom he trusted for guarding him had taken out their knives and were ready for the kill. It was S. Nizam Reddy, the security officer who snatched the keys of the secret vaults of the treasures and handed over the same to prince Mukarram Jah. Mukarram never wanted to take risks since possibility of Nizam coming out of comma could not be ruled out. Ultimately, the great relief came to the Nizam when he breathed his last on 24th February 1967, and proceeded to meet his God.

Sadly, the things did not end with his death. It is reliably learnt that other personal guards of Nizam were instantly removed and replaced by Andhra Pradesh police personnel. No chance was taken as Nizam was guarded by most loyal and trustworthy persons and they could always spill the beans any time later which could not only cause embarrassment to the prince but would have also brought to the notice of the public the unfortunate developments taking place in the palace.

The entire script of treachery and betrayal was authored by Princess DURRASHAWAR, the mother of prince Mukarram Jah. She harboured maximum hatred for the Nizam, since her husband the real crown prince of the Kingdom was disinherited by the Nizam. The electricity of the palace was cut off and the valuables of the treasure transferred to various secret locations in Hyderabad by Prince Mukarram Jah.

Mukkaram Jah was crowned as Nizam the VIII on 6th April, 1967. I am at my wits end to comprehend the significance of such futile exercise since there was no kingdom left for him to govern. It however did give him an authority to deal with the wealth of the Nizam dynasty the way he liked without any challenge from any quarters. I suppose he did amazingly well on this count which we shall witness later.

10

Downward Slide of the Dynasty

Family is the oldest social institution which the mankind has known. It exists even in the animal world in some form or the other even if it is far a short duration. Animal fiercely love their new born, protect them and hone their skills to survive in a hostile geographical and climatic environment. It is further surprising that even animals believe in social harmony and practice 'live and let live' philosophy. It is very seldom that an animal attacks human being unless until provoked.

The institution of the family in human society is however, on an altogether different pedestal. Man is the only animal which can think and speak unlike other animals. It is because of this divine gift that family is the epicenter of development of social groups, clan and evolution of the state. Therefore, it is certain that if the institution of the family is not nurtured it is bound to upset the social harmony's and few delinquent families are sufficient to upset the social order with disastrous consequences.

I have deviated from my main subject, but I am compelled to. We tend to analyse the criminality of an individual only from the legal perspective and are quite elated if a conviction is secured from the courts. In my view, we should study the causes of crimes by conducting scientific studies and make available our findings not only to the law enforcing agencies but also to the groups engaged in the uplift of the society. An independent Bureau could be set up comprising of psychoanalysts, psychiatrists and social scientists to conduct in-depth research to undertake the study of anti-social and criminal behaviour patterns of individuals or group.

Let us recapitulate a true incident. In the beginning of 20th century, a lad with very poor economical background decided to join the French army as his family could not afford his higher education. The boy therefore appeared before the Service Selection Board. The boy was of exceptional natural talent and thus came out with phenomenal but incredible marks in Intelligence Quotient (IQ) Test. Fearing there may have been some error in conducting the tests he was made to undergo the tests again. The results were again the same owing to this extraordinary talents the panel of psychologists inferred that if selected to join the army he shall be a misfit and his behaviour may ultimately prove to be injurious to the health of the fighting institution. The boy was therefore, rejected for commission in the army but the Board wrote a recommendatory letter to the government giving the reasons for rejection and made a strong plea that the state should sponsor his higher education. The French Government honoured their recommendation. Ultimately, this boy was the one who was in the team of nuclear scientists who carried out the successful operation of the atomic explosion. We know this boy by the name of OTTO HAHN. It therefore, logically follows that we cannot afford to be stereotyped in our thinking if we want to develop a cohesive and harmonious family and society. We do not find any other example of such out of the box thinking in any other selection boards of the armed forces in the world.

After having reached to this stage of my investigative journey, I was compelled to think and understand the reasons which could be the cause of the irrational behviour of certain members of the family of the Nizam which was the main reasons for the conflict and disintegration of family and consequently the steep fall in their reputation. After all the two grandsons of the Nizam were highly educated having post-graduate degrees from the Oxford and Cambridge Universities. These two individuals were also fortunate enough to be born into the family of one of the richest man in he world. Mukarram was in line for being crowned the VIIIth Nizam in case Indian independence had got delayed. Mukarram, in fact could never get rid of the hangover of the past glory and lived in a make-believe world. His distorted ambitions and greed had injurious influence on his mind set and he had no respect for the law or any regard for the traditional values of the family. In fact, Mukarram could never reconcile to the changing political contours of the independent India.

Prince Mukarram Jah was crowned as the VIIIth Nizam on 6th April, 1967 in violation of the established practice that consequent upon the death of the ruler, the next senior most in the blood line adores the throne. The legitimate rights of Prince Muazzam Jah Bahadur, the younger sons of the VIIth Nizam should have been crowned notwithstanding the fact that he had no male issue but was totally ignored of this symbolic honour. The world coronation as per Webster Encylopaedic dictionary of English language means "ceremony of crowning a king or queen or other sovereign". He was neither a king nor was there any kingdom to be ruled. With this coronation ceremony he also unashamedly inherited the titles of "His exalted highness the Rustam of the Age, the Aristotle of the times, Ruler of the Kingdom Asif Jah VIII, the conqueror of dominons, the regulation of the Realm, faithful Ally of the British Government to his name. All these items were given by the Britishers to the then ruling Nizam, i.e., his grandfather who had died. In the present context, these titles were misappropriated. This can best we illustrated by the following true incident.

After the 1965 war, our Prime Minister was in London to attend the Commonwealth Conference, on the side lines the President of Pakistan accused India for triggering the war in the Rann of *Kutch* (Gujarat State). Lal Bahadur Shastri in his usual inimitable style humbly replied "Mr. President you are a field marshal and I know nothing about the military matters but one thing I am sure that even a Havaldar of our Indian army would not make that mistake".

No sooner Mukarram Jah was crowned than barely a few days thereafter three auctioneers from the Southby firm of London visited Hyderabad and went back on 4th May, 1967. The purpose of their visit needs no guessing but it is certain that the ground work to auction the two gigantic gold coins had begun. Police authorities in Hyderabad also closely monitored the visits of these foreigners. The police in their report in May 1968 indicated that Mukarram Jah was in possession of gigantic coins of Akbar weighing 1600 Totals (18 kg 560 gms) and 800 golas (nine kg 280 gms). We do not know the source of their information but it may be true because such treasurers were never disclosed to the authorities. There is a possibility that these coins although made of solid gold but may not have been necessarily the *Nazrana* coins (gift) since during the reign of Akbars no gift coins of that weight were ever minted. Police report further indicated that an Iranian national from Bombay named AGAI HUSSAIN HEMMTI met the prince to negotiate the price of the rare gold coins on behalf of a private buyer from the United States, who was prepared to pay 20 lakh dollars. (Two million dollars). The middle man was however, informed that the offer will be considered. The Prince thought that these coins could fetch a better price and therefore, sent him back and paid him Rs. 5000 towards his personal expenses incurred by him during the visit.

Central Excise Authorities also were monitoring the developments and asked the Financial Advisor whether the Nizam was in possession of the primary gold or gold coins on the day of his demise. The Financial Advisor gave an evasive reply and stated vide his letter in August, 1967 that the Nizam had sold all his primary gold, *asharfis*, sovereigns as early as 1950 and the remainder was donated to the Government in October 1966 to augment the war efforts. He also stated in his letter that it will be very difficult for the present Nizam (Prince Mukarram Jah) to state categorically that his late grandfather had no primary gold or gold coins, etc., and requested that at least six months period be given to ascertain the facts. No reply was however, ever given to the Central Excise Authorities which was the designated authority to administer the gold control rules. The Financial Advisor could not give me any satisfactory reply to justify his serious omission.

The sequence of these events, just after the expiry of mourning period of the Nizam's death clearly indicates that the Nizam did conceal, the substantial amount of primary gold even after donating 411 (against 425 kg promised) kgs to the Government. It is also proved that the two gigantic gold coins which were listed for auction and are subject matter of our enquiry were part of the gold intended for donation by the Nizam as the portion of gold which consisted of coins, *ashrafis* and coins of numismatic value were deliberately withheld. Mukkaram Jah was fully aware that in due course in the near future the rare historical gift coins will generate astronomical wealth. But he also understood that numerous enforcement agencies were closely watching his moves and it was no easy task to translate his dreams into reality and at the same time get away with it. He must have been discretely working out a more sophisticated *modus operandi* to pursue his goals. He thus finally flew out of India to London in May 1968. As his plane soared high into the sky the downward slide of the dynasty had begun.

11

The Crisis of Identity

During my informal chats with the financial advisor. I gathered a very interesting fact. He informed me that whenever the grandsons of the Nizam visited Delhi, the then Prime Pandit J.L. Nehru insisted that they stayed in Teen Murti House, the official residence of the Prime Minister instead in the Ashoka Hotel where they usually checked in. Whether, true or otherwise, but as our late Prime Minister was a great Philosopher — Statesman, who wrote poetry using the prose medium, his compassion for others is understandable and there is nothing strange about it. They were also given an option for being co-opted in the Indian Foreign Service. It may be true because we were short of the bureaucrats in the elite service and many talented persons were opted-out during that period in the service. Further, with their academic qualifications and past background they would have really made an excellent bureaucrat. It is also possible that the Financial Advisor was just trying to intimidate me by flaunting such story so that I kept Mukarram Jah out of my radar.

Courtesy and kindness flowing from the most unexpected quarters to an individual is really a boon and a huge debt too and has to be paid back in equal measure to the benefactor. But it was not to be. I suppose the grandsons of Nizam suffered from an acute intellectual diarrhoea. In the army, we have a tradition that a Senior officer addresses his Junior Officer by his first name and his rank is never prefixed to his name. It promotes comradeship and mutual affection as well. I did witness an exception to this established tradition while I was under training in the Indian Military Academy, Dehradun, Major Bhawani Singh was our adjutant. He always came to the Parade Ground in a horse driven *bagghi* (carriage) charioting himself. He was always addressed Major Maharaj Kumar Bhawani Singh by the Commandant of the Academy who was a two-star general. It was neither incumbent upon the general to do so nor the Major expected it. But it was genuine courtesy and kindness which deeply touched him and he accepted it considering it as a debt to be paid back later. This gentleman officer paratrooper who was voluntarily drawing a salary of one rupee per month from the Government got himself air dropped behind the enemy lines in the 1965 war and brought laurels to his regiment and earned Mahavir Chakra for himself. He retired as a Brigadier to settle down in his erstwhile Princely State of Jaipur. It is unfortunate that he is no more with us and departed on his final journey in 2011. He did succeed in teaching us as to how kindness and Courtesy should be paid back with due interest on the debt. Grandsons of Nizam however, failed to do so instead choose a self-defeating path.

The Nizams had an apartment in London where the mother of Mukarram Jah shifted with the younger son sometimes after the coronation ceremony. Nothing is known with regard to the activities of her younger son except that he was not engaged in any kind of activity except that he was idling his time. Thus it was DURRASHWAR, the mother who was still calling the shots and controlled the family. She had no choice since she was determined to take the grand betrayal to the logical end. It is thus in London that the future course of action was taking shape. By now, they must have fully realised that with stringent laws of England and its equally efficient law enforcing agencies it was bound to become the biggest impediment in their illicit activities and therefore it was imperative to shift Mukarram Jah operational base to some remote corner of the globe where more favourable conditions were obtained. With this end in view, Australia was chosen the next destination for Mukkaram to pursue their dreams.

He accordingly migrated to Perth in Western Australia sometime in 1971. Besides acquiring the residential property he also purchased two lakhs hectares of land, four hundred miles from Perth with the ostensible ploy of sheep breeding. It was definitely an intelligent move to provide a perfect smoke screen for his clandestine activities.

Before he would settle down in Australia, his Turkish born wife Esra gave him the shock of his life. She refused to join him in his business and told him bluntly that she had married a Prince and not a shepherd and sought the divorce. The couple was ultimately separated legally in the year 1980. Deserted by his wife, he was now a lonely man, thousands of miles away from his homeland but he never gave up. He fell in love with his personal assistant, an Australian citizen named Helen Sommon and married her. The tragedy did not allow him the peace of mind which he needed desperately and even his second wife died of AIDS a few years later. The bliss of bed chamber always betrayed him. He married yet another Manglya Onur a former Miss Turkey who also left him. She along with her daughter Niloufer now claim to inherit to huge share of Nizam property.

When someone chooses a path knowing well that it shall lead only to shame and disgrace he also unwittingly destroys the bridges en route and seals his own escape route for any possible retreat. This is what exactly happened to Mukarram Jah. He purchased a decommissioned mine sweeper of the Australian Navy in an auction and converted it into a commercial vessel. Mine Sweepers are battleships of medium size and weight and are used by naval forces which shall ahead of an advancing flotilla to clear the passage of sea mines laid by the enemy. After statutory years of service these ships are decommissioned and are sent either to a scrap yard or auctioned.

Mukarram recruited one Andrew Chhaderton, a notorious drug-trafficker to Captain the Ship. It is not known as to which sea routes they followed or the countries of their visits and also the exact nature of their activities which were of course always suspect. It is quite possible since there are no statutory regulatory bodies to monitor their voyage in the high Seas. We have already witnessed the landing of the Pakistani Terrorist in Bombay in November, 2008 which resulted in the loss of hundreds of innocent lives. It is purely because of the fact such tragedies occur as there is no system in place to give us an advance warning of such violations by sea routes unlike the air space violations which are immediately noticed by the Air Traffic Controllers. It is indeed a mystery as to what was the real motive of launching an ocean going commercial ship. But I suppose he remembered well the maxim of the great historian

K.M. Panikkar who said "the one who rules the waves, shall rule the land also". Any beginning is always small and it is not without a reason that he purchased a discarded. Minesweeper which is a fast ocean going ships. And can withstand the choppy seas and have much better manoeuvring capabilities. The maritime laws in relation to a sea-going vessel beyond the exclusive Economic Zone of a country are virtually non-existent and it gives a long rope to tile strategcians who prefer sea routes. Even our past visionary leaders visualised the importance of the Navy and Shivaji, the great Maratha Warrior raised his navy under Kanhoji Angre. The race continues even today. The United States has an entire fleet of Naval ship located in the Middle East and China is in a desperate mood to have a foothold in Myanmar (Burma) and even in Pakistan. It would therefore be risky to infer that he had purchased the Ship only for gold or narcotic smuggling. We should not forget that Island Nation of Singapore was once a piece of marshy land inhabited by mosquitoes. The people of even today purchase uninhabited islands although purpose of such ownership of such pieces of land really cannot easily be understood.

In Perth, the Prince also developed a close working association with ARPAD Security Agency who always employed ex-members of the Special Air Service Regiments. This security agency was already in the suspect list of Australian Intelligence Agencies as they were involved in smuggling of gold from one country to another. In all probabilities the personnel of the vessel purchased by Mukarram may have been drawn from this agency as it mutually benefitted both the parties. He thus easily got the trained and robust men to man the ship which was so essential to carry out his illegal pursuits safely.

Mukarram realised that generating illegal money alone was not sufficient to enjoy such wealth since such money can be seized or appropriated by the law enforcing agencies. This ill-gotten money had to be converted into the legitimate earning which in popular parlance is called White Money. He therefore became the Director of an Australian Firm functioning under the name and style of Herbros Australia-based in Perth. The only one shareholder of this company is Herbros Establishment PO Box 34605, Caduz, Liechtenstein. The other Director of Herbros Australia in Perth is one Jean Paul Crosier of Rue Ceard, Geneva, Switzerland. Mukarram was therefore, suspected to be bringing money from India to Australia through Herbros Establishment which is quite evident considering the number of visits he made to Switzerland.

After his death, Haji Mastan, a doyen of smugglers fraternity had a total accumulated wealth of Rs. 500 crore (50 millions) from his illicit activities, so was the estimation of Indian Intelligence Agencies. By present day reckoning it may run into thousands of crores. But after his death only two visible properties were noticed on his name, there was one flat in London and the other on Pedder Road in Mumbai and the rest of the wealth just disappeared. But modern economic offenders are not only shrewd but intelligent also. They use sophisticated banking channels for laundering the money and post the wealth in their own accounts. No one can easily trace the source of such money and at the same time it never disappears. That is what Dawood Ibrahim Kasgar is doing by cozily sitting in a well-protected bungalow in Clifton in Karachi.

Mukarram thus proceeded on very scientific lines. Firstly, the infrastructure was well laid by purchasing huge mass of land for sheep breeding, a perfect cover for illicit activities. Purchase of sea going ship for the ostensible purpose of commercial activities and recruitment of tainted personnel clearly expose his intentions. By joining the money laundering firms he ensured that illegal money was indeed earned through legitimate business transactions. He left nothing to chance but no one knows how far he has succeeded. With the close co-operation of numerous law enforcing agencies of the world, his activities however could not got undetected for a long time. But one thing is however, certain that he did succeed in ample measure to flutter away not only the treasurers of the Nizam but also the goodwill and image which the ruling dynasty had created during their seven generations rule in Telangana region namely Hyderabad State.

12

Social Consequences of False Ego of Caste Consciousness

It is not without reasons that I am devoting a chapter on the ego of Caste Consciousness. In fact, the disintegration of the royal family of Hyderabad and its subsequent misadventures with the Nizams wealth have a strong socio-psychological angle.

Stratification of the Caste Systems in human society was indeed born of false ego and it is perpetrated and cemented through the ages by those who could manipulate the social system. During the pre-historical periods the Caste System did exist but it was not so rigid so as to create any social problems. Emergence of Rishi Vyas and Valmiki amply demonstrates that there was upward mobility of the caste status and even matrimonial alliances were also forged considering the numerous factors other than the cast. At some point in our history, the system became so rigid that it is threatening the social system now, it is also a fact that India and Pakistan are worst affected by this malady.

Economic compulsions of the later part of the 20th century did give us the impression that the caste system would ultimately wither away. Unfortunately, the system has again been revived and the reasons thereof need not be told as it is too obvious and evident to merit any narration.

I had a Muslim colleague who had a daughter of marriageable age. I was taken aback when he once told me that he will never marry his daughter in certain Muslim caste. It was very surprising because theoretically caste has no relevance in the Muslim religion. I had another Christian colleaghe, whose name was Prabhu Pinto. I asked him why his first name was synonymous with a Hindu God and he told me that his ancestors were Hindu Brahmin from Goa before they converted into the Christianity few hundred years back therefore they continue to retain their caste.

I had the occasion to go through the pay books of the slain Pakistani Muslim soldiers after the 1965 war, and was totally surprised to know that besides religion it also had the column for the caste. Many pay books revealed that although the religion of the dead soldier was a Muslim but he was from the Rajput Caste. No wonder the illustrious family of Bhuttos of Pakistan always claimed that they were Rathore Rajputs. Back home the cruel judgements of *Khaap Panchayats* in Western UP awarding death penalty without any remorse to persons marrying outside caste is equally disturbing.

The ego always cripples the mental health but false ego destroys the personality forever. Mughals may have been class conscious but their matrimonial alliances were never influenced by any caste considerations. They never looked towards Samarkand for a bride. No wonder during the few centuries rule they never witnessed any palace intrigues. We do find an exception in Aurengzeb who sowed the seed of Mughal decline but his personality traits were born out of his own myopic view of history and intellectual infirmities. In complete contrast, the Nizams looked towards Turkey for matrimonial alliances. Not only his elder son, the Crown Prince was marred in Turkey but his grandson Mukarram was married to Esra in Turkey. Nizams could not find a girl of their caste in India although they ruled the State for roughly two centuries.

The two ladies brought with them the huge wealth of false ego of their caste which was sufficient enough to tear apart the cohesiveness of the family. To buttress my argument, let us recapitulate as to what she said to her husband when he had shifted to Australia to start Sheep Breeding activities. To seek the divorce from her husband who was still claiming to be VIIIth Nizam, she simply said she had married a Prince and not a shepherd. Such was the intensity of her false ego of caste consciousness.

We do not know the background of these two Ladies in Turkey, but it appears they must have been close relations as they worked together in close to co-operation to have enormous influence on the fortunes or the misfortunes of the dynasty.

Life never unfolds itself according to a written script. There are numerous factors, social, economical and political which decide the course of destiny. More than these factor the individuals' perverse thinking has a more decisive impact in precipitating the dooms day. The duo of daughter-in-law Princess Durrashwar and grand-daughter-in-law Princess Esra were sufficient to destroy the fortunes of the ruling family. Princess Durrashwar never forgave the late Nizam for disinheriting her husband thus eliminating her for ever from becoming a future Queen. This provoked her to foist her elder son Mukarram as the future King of the ruling dynasty and Princess ESRA too dreamed to be a future Queen.

Overbearing influence of Princess Durrashwar for her own vested interested alienated other members of the family and caused resentment and frustration in them. Favourable conditions existed for my friends from Media to earn the sympathy of such disgruntled person to become our informant. In sptie of these positive developments the mole was mortally scared of his own personal safety. Further he continued to be a beneficiary to the luxuries of Nizam's left over fortunes which could be seriously jeopardised. Even my frequent visits to Hyderabad was causing anxiety to the Financial Advisor as his employment was certain only if he was loyal and trustworthy to Mukkaram. Though he was turning cold feet yet I found him cooperative albeit resitatingly. Our mole however, came forward provided he was given anonymity and we had no problems with such pre-condition. Our meeting took place with all precautionary measures against exposure of the source.

It was revealed during the interactive session that the late Nizam was in possession of the two huge Nazraria Coins of Mugal Era which was slated for the auction besides other high value gold coins. The Nizam was always apprehensive that these may be removed secretly for clandestine sale because of their antique value. He, therefore, never parted with the keys of treasure chests where these were carefully stored. Mukarram was aware of it and therefore the first thing he did when Nizam slipped into 'comma' was to remove the keys even before he had breathed his last.

Consequent upon Nizam death, the trusted security apparatus around Nizam was immediately replaced by the State Police who had no clue with regard to strong and dangerous under currents of intrigues and betrayals' in the family. He did not stop at that and even electricity and water supply was cut off to ensure that persons entrusted with the removal of the treasure could not be identified and their activities could go on unnoticed The source further revealed that it may be recalled that the Nizam had pledged 425 kgs. of Gold to be donated which consisted of 411 kgs of solid Gold and the rest being in the form of Coins. But in actual fact only solid Gold was given as a donation and the Coins were embezzled. When Nizam realised the embezzlement he conveyed his displeasure to everyone in the family gathering. Although Nizam wore no Crown now but he could never reconcile to such open defiance of his authority. The bunch of the keys of the treasure chest had thus become the integral part of his body. The magnitude of the cruel betrayal penetrated the bones of Nizam and he became a bundle of nerves and with it his journey to the grave had just begun.

Mukarram was a very knowledgeable person and he was fully aware that the priceless treasures which the Nizam had left would one-day fetch astrnomical value in the international market. He was also aware the entire treasure was the subject matter of the Gold Control Act and Antiquities Exports Control Act, and violation of any of these laws would render him liable not only for fine but also imprisonment which he could ill-afford. Utmost secrecy was therefore, needed to remove these treasures to any foreign destination. Time clock of his mind was therefore ticking very fast. The mole explained to me in great detail that the two Gold Coins were surreptiously mixed with the unaccompanied baggage of a renowned personality of Hyderabad who was visiting London for medical consultation of his wife who was suspected to be suffering from Cancer sometimes in between 1967 to 1972. The two Coins prima facie appear to have been stored in the Apartment in London where Princess Durrashwar was living. This piece of information shifting blame on someone to have taken out these Coins appear to be false and has been deliberately dished out to shield himself from any fall out of his disclosures. To me it appeared to be unconvincing for the simple reason that Nizam family still commanded respect amongst people as well as in bureaucracy and Mukarram himself would have undertaken the safe transportation of the valuable without any hindrance or hassle. Whatever, may be the real truth, the complicity of Mukarram is well-established.

The next information given by the mole was however, very crucial to identify the perpetrator and define his role in the complicity. Just before the auction was to take place Habib Ansari, the Legal Advisor to Prince along with Personal Secretary to Mukarram were deputed to witness the auction in Geneva. The question arises why should they witness the auction and who authorised them to do so. The normal practice of auctioneers is to withhold the ownership of items being auctioned. By sending these two individuals the secrecy of the stakeholder was clearly breached so was the secrecy of sequence of events of the gigantic Coins from Hyderabad to the auctioneer's table was fully compromised. It may also be noted that when the price of the rare piece of Gold Coins was not being offered by the bidders, the auctioneer's had to buy back the Coins from the highest bidder at a premium to safeguard the financial stakes of the owners. The Legal Advisor had thus a very important role to perform and he did it successfully. Let us see the credentials of the two individuals who went to witness the auction.

Habib Ansari was once a class fellow of Mukarram. Though a qualified lawyer he was virtually an exclusive advocates to Nizams and had the sole rights of all the briefs to take care of the legal problems not only in India but abroad as well, there is no need to mention that he was not a native of Andhra but was a migrant from Uttar Pradesh. Other details of Ansari are as under:

(i) Height 5 ft. 4 inch to to 5ft. 5 inch

(ii) Age 50 years

(iii) Built Thin built

(iv) Res 8–2–674, Banjara Hills, Hyderabad-3

The other person said to be Secretary to the Prince who accompanied Ansari to Switzerland is Shahid Hussain. He does not have any such qualification to be appointed as Personal Secretary and was virtually a muscleman. He had criminal records against him and probably it was his right qualification for the job. After all it was absolutely essential that he should have accompanied the Legal Advisor considering his fragile frame. Ansari must have been carrying very sensitive documents and was vulnerable to any evil designs of potential adversaries of Mukarram. The other details of Shahid are as under:

(i)	Height	6 Feet
(ii)	Age	40 years
(iii)	Built	Very healthy. To look more ferocious with sported mustaches.
(iv)	Res	3-6-363/1, Liberty Building, Hyderabad-3

The duo were initially booked to the travel to Geneva by Swiss Air, to avoid any suspicion they preferred to travel by Air India and tickets were purchased from India Travel Bureau, Hyderabad. To conceal their identity they even gave a false residential address in their travel documents as Kohe Zareen 10-3-3098, Humayun Nagar, Hyderabad as against the actual residential addresses given in the passport.

It is certain that both had left for London by AI Flight 109 on 6th November, 1987 and the air ticket indicated their travel route as Hyderabad-Bombay-London-Bombay-Hyderabad. As regards to their onward journey from London is not known. Our enquiries in London were of, no avail since Immigration Authorities in U.K. do ask disembarking passengers to file the requisite information but do not ask the outgoing embarking passengers to file the requisite information. British Customs also do not maintain any such records. I am not aware if any procedural changes have come in force in view of the global terrorist threats.

It is not that the citizens of Hyderabad were indifferent to what was happening in the Kings *Kothi*, they were equally worried the way historical treasures were being siphoned off by the descendents of Nizam to satisfy their greed to amass the wealth. It was a very bold step indeed when one Ismail Zabin, editor of the local daily *"Hamare Ikdam"* published an interview from his own intelligence source indicating that Nizam was in possession of the two gigantic Gold Coins in question. In pursuance of this report even the then Collector of Central Excise, Hyderabad interviewed Sahebzadi Pasha, the daughter of Late Nizam, who too confirmed the presence of these Gold Coins. Unfortunately, no one gave much credence to these disclosures and assumed that it was the fallout of personal rivalries within the family that information was being planted.

Such impression gained currency since Sahebzadi Pasha was said to be an illegitimate daughter of Late Nizam. She died in 1985, and had she been alive, she would have been a source of much valuable information.

The meeting with the source ended on a very cordial note with a promise to meet again, should the need arise.

Hitherto a historical distance of approximately three centuries had been covered. On the basis of the published historical evidence and interaction with individuals who were knowledgeable and with no personal interests whosoever it has been irrefutably established that Mughal Emperors had a tradition of minting special Gold Coins of different sizes and weight to commemorate important events of their rule and called these coins "Nazrana Coins". English historians called these coins 'Gigantic Coins'. These coins were usually given to the visiting dignitaries during the occasion of coronation, marriage or to mark the importance of some extraordinary events. Out of these coins, a Nazrana Coin weighing 1000 tolas (11 kg 600 gms) was given to the father of the founder of the Nizam ruling dynasty for a daring rescue operation to save the life of the son of Emperor Aurangzeb as a token of appreciation and gratitude. In all likelihood another gift of 100 Tolas (one kg 160 gms) coins to him may have been given on another occasion which escaped the attention of the person maintaining records of such events simply because of the fact that there is hard evidence to suggest that the Late Nizam was in possession of Gold Coins till the time of his death in February 1967. Unfortunately, these Gold Coins were never revealed by the Nizam when he acceded to Indian Republic and were never disclosed to the Government in any of the mandatory statutory documents.

It is also a fact that Mukarram was in the knowledge of the existence of these coins and also knew that these Gold Coins were part of the Gold pledged by the Nizam to the Government. He secretly got these two coins separated from the lot to be donated. Prima-facie it was an act of theft and embezzlement. No sooner he got himself coronated he started making vigorous efforts to dispose of these coins secretly but could not succeed as the price being offered was much below his estimation.

Notwithstanding these facts discovered during the investigations we had no version of Mukarram which was not only vital but also relevant to cement our arguments.

Mukarram was not only intelligent but great strategician to accomplish his goals. We have to admire his foresight since he meticulously planned his moves a decade in advance and got himself firmly parked in Australia with a fond hope that the arms of Indian Law will not be able to reach him or harm his interests. Sadly, that was not to be. Crime Authority of Australia was smarter than him as we shall see next.

13

And the Truth Prevails

I was really dismayed on learning that since the Andhra State Government had vetoed the investigations into the disappearance of the said historical treasures from the possession of Nizam, I would have to investigate the case. I was fully aware of my own professional limitations and lack of expertise to undertake such mission which essentially was the job of a Police agency. I still cannot figure out the logic of their refusal since the case had an international ramifications. Assuming that had even if the Andhra Police investigated the case they too had to go through the Interpol Wing of the CBI. As per Swiss Authorities to intervene in the matter. The Swiss Government could come into picture only if a clear-cut case of theft or embezzlement was revealed. Further, it had also to be proved that such embezzlement took place only after 1947 when India had become a republic and the State of Nizam had acceded to the Indian Republic. Had the embezzlement taken place before 1947, the Government of India had no *locus-standie* to intervene in the matter. I however, took the challenge considering the fact that in all investigations the basic approach to the subject is fundamentally the same.

As far I know, the CBI is one of the finest institutions we have. I had the proud privilege of working with them in close co-ordination for over a decade during my tenure in the Directorate of Revenue Intelligence and Central Economic Intelligence Bureau. I was also fortunate to have 96-undergone few intense capsule courses on investigations which were conducted by the CBI. It was therefore, really disappointing that the State Government did not have confidence in them. In doing so there must have been, I suspect some political considerations.

With such frustrating experience I am compelled to make a few comments. Firstly, it is high time that the CBI is mandated by the law to have an All India jurisdiction on the pattern of the Federal Bureau of investigations of the United States. They should also be authorised to take up investigations suo motu where they feel cases have serious National and International ramifications.

We have witnessed the Quantum Jump in the field of technology in the past few decades. Gone are the days, when one had to walk a few kilometers to the Post Office to make a phone call from a non-functional instrument. Today even in small villages every family has at least one Mobile Phone. The crime scenario too has undergone a sea change and the criminals make full use of these technological developments to their advantages. The canvas of crime has also enlarged and are no more confined to *Zar-Zoru* and *Zamin*. Cyber Crimes, Banking Frauds, Money Laundering, offences under Narcotics, all have not only caused severe damage to our economy but pose a serious threat to our National Security as well. The State Police Organisations with inadequate 97 staff are just struggling to maintain law and order problems and have little time left to do full justice to the task of serious investigation.

No investigation agency in the World has hundred per cent success rate in crime detection or conviction in the criminal cases. The Courts do not go by the reports appearing in the media or by the intensity of the rumours but take into account the hard evidence marshalled by the investigating agency. Hard evidence is not a commodity which could be purchased from the market and thus requires lots of patience, time and dedication. The criminals are too intelligent today and even before the crime is committed they work out a plan to destroy the evidence, sometimes investigations do fail and we thoughtlessly attribute such failures to some non-exiatent hidden agenda of the Investigating Agency.

I have a very interesting true incident which was narrated to me by a Senior Registrar of a High Court. I am tempted to share it because it clearly brings out the fact that an investigation is not a cake-walk. A few years back a Magistrate was suspended by the Delhi High Court for granting bail at midnight to a notorious smuggler of Silver, who was called Silver King of Delhi. The case was well-contested by the prosecution as well as defending lawyers. On the following day all the newspapers splashed the news under juicy captions to which the Hon'ble High Court did not take kindly and constituted an "Enquiry Authority". I happened to be a party in the case on behalf of the Government and to the best of my knowledge there was nothing wrong in the bail order except that it did hurt my investigative efforts. I approached the Registrar with a request that since prima facie there was no ulterior motive and therefore suspension was too harsh. The Registrar listened to me carefully and thanked me for my humanitarian approach but narrated a true incident with a suggestion that after listening to him, I may change my opinion. The incident as narrated by him is produced below.

During the British Rule a Judicial Magistrate in erstwhile Madhya Bharat (now Madhya Pradesh) acquired notoriety for discharging his duties for monetary considerations. The Government therefore deputed an outstanding inspector of the Criminal Investigation Department to investigate the case and submit his report within a month. The investigating officer attended the Court *incognito* and made discreet enquiries from all possible sources and submitted the report to the Government exonerating the Magistrate from the charges. To his surprise and horror the Inspector got his suspension order for dereliction of duty on the following day.

The poor inspector had no choice but to approach the Magistrate directly to ascertain as to what was the truth. The Magistrate too was frank in admitting that he indeed had been corrupt but refused to divulge as to how he succeeded in his *Modus-Operandi*. He was however, liberal enough to promise that the day he retired from the service he himself will call on the inspector and tell him how he succeeded in hoodwinking the law. He also promised the inspector that in case he retired earlier he could come and know the truth. After narrating the incident, the Registrar impressed upon me that the investigation of a case is not all that simple as it is made out to be by the onlookers and at times the facts slip away without our knowledge and the results had gone awry.

It is difficult to understand that wherever it suits the political compulsions of a State Government, the CBI is given a green signal to undertake the investigation otherwise they are denied to undertake their legitimate professional obligations. Some activists want to bring the CBI under The Right to Information Act. Another bunch of the activists are canvassing for bifurcating the CBI and attach its Economic Offence Wing with the Lokpal and Lokayukta.

These activists fail to understand that the investigation is a very vital component of the intelligence craft and the whole structure is an integrated medium. No investigation can be taken to a logical end unless until it has positive inputs from the intelligence gathering and effective surveillance. In a democracy we can definitely play around with institutions but then we should be prepared to face ill-consequences of such fantasy. There is a proverb in colloquial language in eastern part of Uttar Pradesh which runs like this *"Jaun rahi Kulhari Maa dhar, wahi laiga narayan lohar"* (Whatever the sharpness was in the axe same has been taken away by Narayan iron Smith). Instead of revamping and strengthening the institutions we are hell-bent upon to destroy it. An American Sociologist while talking about the social change states that Karl Marx belongs to that category of saints who by their vision change the world but do not find the changed world according to their vision. Assuming but not admitting that our activists are Karl Marx's one an safely conclude that their vision is definitely lacking strategic thinking notwithstanding their genuine concern if any.

The truth has ultimately prevailed owing to the efforts of the CBI failing which I would have never succeeded in my mission. It is because of their rapport and healthy professional relationship with the Crime Authority of Australia, that mystery of missing Gold Coins of Mughal Era from the treasures of Nizam has been solved. The defence of the CBI by me may be purely because of the anguish I have been undergoing by witnessing the thoughtless assault on a robust and efficient Institution from certain quarters is definitely unwarranted.

Crime Authority of Australia is the counterpart of our CBI in Australia and both are members of Interpol with Headquarters in France. We find excellent co-operation with each other in relation to detection of crime and other related assistance on the subject. Crime Authority of Australia enjoys sufficient freedom of action which has very conducive bearing on the crime health of that country. It is high time we too inculcate the same degree of trust in our own Institutions by giving them free-hand to act in the interest of the security and integrity of the nation.

I vividly recall the conversation with the Director General of State Archives, who told me without mincing his words that even a Rickshaw Puller in the Hyderabad City knows as to who had taken out the missing gigantic Gold Coins out of India but no one will open his mouth. It seems the common man is still paranoid with the past glory of the Nizam. Under the circumstances, it was absolutely necessary to know from the horse's mouth as to what he had to say about the missing Gold Coins. Accordingly, the Australian Authority was requested to take necessary follow-up action by the CBI.

Consequent upon settling down in Australia and immediately acquiring huge immoveable property besides his lavish life-style Mukarram Jah was already in the scanner of the Australian Intelligence Agencies and they had already covered a long distance. Details of their findings have already figured in our earlier chapters. It gave the Australian Authorities a perfect alibi to take up the investigations further.

The palatial residential premises of Mukarram Jah in Perth were visited by the Officers of the Crime Authority of Australia in December, 1987. His house was like a fort concealed by very high walls, to make it, still more inaccessible, Concertina Coils were placed on high walls. The residence had been fitted with all necessary gadgets to give the early warning of any intruder. Needless to say, the residence was well-guarded by Private Security Guards. 'Mukarram Jah was confronted with the photographs of the two gigantic Gold Coins listed for auction. Surprisingly he was graceful in admitting that he had seen the two coins in Hyderabad in the valuable treasure chest of the Nizam. Simultaneously, he was intelligent enough to state that he had directed the then Financial Advisor to sell or dispose off the coins the way he liked. It has been a deliberate ploy since the Financial Advisor to whom he was referring to had died in 1968 and dead men do not speak. It is a fact that although he had settled in Australia yet he did visit Hyderabad from time to time to safeguard his assets from any possible misappropriation. The sustained investigations into the auction of the valuable historical coins must have been in his knowledge. No wonder he shifted the entire blame of embezzlement on a person who was no more available to testify. It is also a fact that the existence of these coins was kept a closely guarded secret with a view to dispose of the same at a later date at an astronomical value. The then Financial Advisor was not a naive to follow a disastrous advise in which he had no stakes and was knowledgeable enough to understand the consequences of such ill advice.

Odysseus adventures to return home after the Trojan War came to an end after ten years and Homer must have been a relieved man to close his epic poem. Our wandering however, is likely to begin again when these historical treasures appear again for auction at some point of time in future. In reality, the journey is not going to end soon.

Index

H

I

J

N